LET MY PRAYER
RISE TO GOD

LET MY PRAYER
RISE TO GOD

A Spirituality for
Praying the Psalms

WILLIAM O. PAULSELL

CHALICE
PRESS

ST. LOUIS, MISSOURI

Cover art: Detail from "Kalayaan" (Freedom) by Edicio de la Torre, from IMAGE, published by Asian Christian Art Association, vol. 85, Dec., 2000
Cover and interior design: Elizabeth Wright
Art direction: Elizabeth Wright

This book is printed on acid-free, recycled paper.

Visit Chalice Press on the World Wide Web at
www.chalicepress.com

10 9 8 7 6 5 4 3 2 1   02 03 04 05 06 07

Library of Congress Cataloging–in–Publication Data

Paulsell, William O.
    Let my prayer rise to God : a spirituality for praying the Psalms/ William O. Paulsell.
        p.   cm.
    ISBN 0-8272-2133-9 (alk. paper)
    1. Bible. O.T. Psalms—Devotional use. I. Title.
BS1430.55 .P38 2002
242'.5—dc21
                                                          2002002068
                                                              CIP

Printed in the United States of America

Contents

Introduction

As Christians, we believe that God is present: in the world, in the church, in our own lives, in human interaction. However, we don't often experience that presence. We may have a deep longing for God, but that divine presence eludes us. We keep hoping for some experience, some encounter with God, that will confirm our faith, but nothing of that nature seems to happen.

The problem, of course, is that we are so distracted. With modern means of communication, we are literally bombarded with input. Advertisers use very sophisticated methods to convince us that we cannot be happy, fulfilled, or socially acceptable people unless we buy the right products. We are told that people will judge us by the cars we drive, the clothes we wear, and the use of the right body care products. Of course, we can be perfectly happy without most of the things people try to sell us, but we are pressured to think otherwise.

At election time, politicians try to convince us that they alone have the truth, and that if we vote for them, our local, state, or national problems will be solved. If we are not inclined to vote for them, we have certain ideological labels affixed to us that imply that there must be something wrong with our character.

We face peer pressure, pressure from our employers, family responsibilities, and community expectations. Is it any wonder that we have a hard time sensing God's presence? How can we break through all these distractions to a clean, clear awareness of God at work in our lives?

Over the centuries, many Christians have engaged in a variety of spiritual disciplines as a way of overcoming distractions. People have fasted, gone into solitude, and practiced various forms of self-denial. Some have taken up the monastic life; others have immersed themselves in social service; and many have tried to develop deep prayer lives.

Prayer is not an easy activity. Some folks have decided to set aside a certain amount of time for prayer each day, fifteen or thirty minutes, even an hour. The first thirty seconds go pretty well, but then the individual is left with a significant amount of time on his or her hands and does not know what to do with it. The whole experience can become frustrating and boring, and is soon given up. The possibility of a rich life of prayer is lost.

In this book I would like to suggest a way of praying that can become a foundation for a deeper prayer life and a way of focusing on God that can help break through many of the distractions that we face every day.

When I was a seminary student back in the 1950s, professor Bard Thompson took students each year to spend a day at the Abbey of Gethsemani in Kentucky. It is one of the most famous monasteries in the world, partly because of the fact that one of its monks was Thomas Merton, a major twentieth-century spiritual writer, whose auto-biography, *The Seven Storey Mountain*, has influenced countless numbers of people. In a conversation with one of the monks, a student asked for guidance on how to develop a deeper prayer life. The monk replied, "Do what we do. Pray the psalms."

The liturgical life of that monastery is very rich. Seven times a day, beginning at 3:15 a.m. and ending around 8:00 p.m., the monks gather in their church to pray. The form of prayer they use is to chant the psalms in the Old Testament. Over a two-week cycle the monks chant all one hundred and fifty psalms. That is the foundation of their prayer lives. This has been a practice since the beginning of the monastic tradition in the early centuries of Christianity. In fact, the *Rule of Saint Benedict,* one of the most widely used of all monastic rules, prescribes praying the entire Psalter every week.

Praying the psalms has been one of the most universally practiced spiritual disciplines. In the middle ages, wealthy laity had *Books of Hours,* which had the psalms arranged for prayer at different times of the day. These books, copied by hand, are now treasured for their artistic qualities. Pages were often illustrated with colorful designs or small scenes appropriate to the psalms. Today many people make use of breviaries, which are collections of psalms, hymns, prayers, and readings for night, morning, midday, afternoon, and evening times of prayer.

Martin Luther described the Psalter as "a kind of school and exercise for the disposition of the heart."[1] Dietrich

---

[1] Martin Luther, *Luther's Works*, vol. 14, ed. Jaroslav Pelikan and Daniel E. Poellot (St. Louis: Concordia Publishing House, 1958), 310.

Bonhoeffer, the German pastor and professor executed by the Nazis, called the psalms "the great school of prayer. Here one learns, first, what prayer means."[2] Matthew Kelty, a Trappist monk, approaches the psalms in terms of what they can teach us about ourselves.

> The psalms can teach us of the conflict with evil within us, bring us face to face with the traitor in our own heart: the two-timer, the time-server, the false friend. Who has not met the demon of envy, of jealousy, of greed, of hatred, lurking in the dark shadows of his depths, a side that rarely comes into the light? And what appropriate words we find in the psalms to deal with these elements of hell within us![3]

As these statements imply, the psalms reflect the best and the worst in us. They speak of deep desire for God and lofty aspirations to live in direct communion with God. They also express anger, vengeance, and hostility, all very human emotions. They force us to face the reality of who we are, and they give us the language to express longing for God and the desire for new life. Praying the psalms on a regular basis will take us through the whole range of human emotions. They are both earthy and mystical, exalted and angry. We can identify with their humanity and are inspired by their spirituality.

The book of Psalms was the prayer book of ancient Israel, and it has served as the prayer book of the church. It has provided the texts for liturgy, hymn, anthem, and cantata. The book constitutes a primer for public worship and a devotional guide for private prayer. It also calls for social justice, challenging us to meet the needs of widows,

---

[2]Dietrich Bonhoeffer, *Life Together* (New York: Harper and Row, 1954), 47.
[3]Matthew Kelty, *Sermons in a Monastery: Chapter Talks by Matthew Kelty* (Kalamazoo, Mich.: Cistercian Publications, 1983), 12–13.

orphans, prisoners, and the oppressed. Although I am suggesting ways to use psalms in your personal prayer life, ancient Israelites understood prayer to be a communal activity. They did it together, often going to Jerusalem for various celebrations, since it was the religious center of the nation. Private prayer should not be seen as a substitute for communal prayer in a religious community. Praying together with other people of faith is an important part of the spiritual growth process.

Like many medieval exegetes, I intend to interpret the psalms on the basis of the Christian gospel, even though they were written before the time of Jesus. Some of them cannot be read without Christ's coming into our minds, Psalm 22 being the most obvious example. In the preface to his translation of the Psalms, Luther wrote

> Would you see the holy Christian Church painted in living color and form and put in one little picture? Then take up the Psalter and you have a fine bright, pure mirror that will show you what the Church is; nay, you will find yourself also in it...and God Himself, besides, and all creatures.[4]

Many of the psalms make reference to the history of Israel. That history began, probably in the 1200s B.C.E., when a motley band of slaves escaped from their captivity in Egypt and moved eastward across the Sinai to Palestine, or, as it was known then, the land of Canaan. These people believed that this land had been promised to their patriarchal ancestors—Abraham, Isaac, and Jacob—who would have lived in the 1700s B.C.E. With some difficulty these people conquered Canaan and lived for a time as a

---

[4]Martin Luther, *Works of Martin Luther,* vol. 6, Board of Publication, United Lutheran Church in America (Philadelphia: Muhlenberg Press, 1932), 388.

confederacy of twelve tribes led, when the need arose, by people called judges. Eventually, a central government was seen as necessary to survival, and a series of kings—Saul, David, and Solomon—established a monarchy that brought some unity and stability. After Solomon a civil war erupted, and the nation was divided. The northern section, consisting of ten tribes, kept the name Israel. The southern part was called Judah.

The weakened nations went into a decline that the religious prophets attributed to their unfaithfulness to God. The northern nation fell to the Assyrians in 722 B.C.E. The people were carried into exile and never heard from again. The southern nation lasted longer, but it fell to the Babylonians in 587 B.C.E., and the population was deported to Babylonia. Here people had to live far away from their homeland and their religious center. Around 520 B.C.E. the people of Judah, the Jews, were allowed to return to Palestine, though many decided to stay where they were. The returnees began rebuilding the temple and worked to restore their worship traditions.

This story is repeated in several of the psalms. Psalm 78, for example, tells the story from the exodus to the reign of David. It vividly describes the faithlessness of the people, even after God had rescued them from slavery. Psalms 80, 81, 83, 105, and 106 also tell the story of the nation's origins and troubles. Although some of the psalms are grounded in specific historical remembrances, they deal with the universal human realities of faithlessness and ingratitude.

In the form in which we now have it, the Psalter is the product of the community of ancient Israel after the exile in Babylonia. Some scholars refer to it as the hymnbook of the Second Temple, that is, the temple the people rebuilt after their return from exile in the sixth century B.C.E. However, it may not have reached final form until the second century B.C.E. Psalm 137 ("By the rivers of Babylon—there we sat down and there we wept" [v. 1]) is a clear reference to the Babylonian exile, indicating that psalms were still being composed by that date. Scholarly studies indicate that some were written well before that. With a few exceptions, it is impossible to date the writing of the psalms with much precision at all, but it is likely that they were composed over a period of many centuries. It does seem clear that they were intended for public worship, and many had obvious liturgical uses.

There are a few strange things about the Psalter. For example, Psalms 14 and 53 are virtually the same. So are 40:14–17 and 70:2–5; 57:7–11 and 108:1–5; and 60:5–12 and 108:6–13. The meaning of some of the terminology is not clear. For example, in some psalms we often find the word *selah*. It was probably a liturgical or musical notation, but no one is sure. Psalm 56 has an editorial notation, "To the leader: according to The Dove on Far-off Terebinths." A terebinth is a tree. Is this a reference to people who are far away?

Most scholars seem to think that the psalms were designed for corporate use, even though many of them are written in the singular first person. Some speak of processions, the temple, and the enthronement of kings. There are psalms of praise, of confession, of lament, of thanksgiving. There are psalms that praise the Law, such as 119, the longest in the Psalter. Some praise Mount Zion as the residence of God. Psalm 45 is a wedding psalm. Some, such as 67 and 136, have repetitive lines that could have been liturgical responses. The Psalter, in short, is a rich feast of a wide variety of praises and prayers that can serve as the foundation of one's devotional life.

At some point, psalms began to be grouped together. Psalms 3–41 and 51–72 are among those attributed to

David. Two groups of psalms are supposed to be from two guilds of temple musicians: the Asaphites, 50 and 73–83, and the Korahites, 42–49; 84–85; 87–88. Psalms 72 and 127 supposedly came from Solomon, and Psalm 90 is described as a prayer of Moses.

Eventually the psalms were arranged into five books. Book 1 consists of Psalms 1–41; Book 2, 42–72; Book 3, 73–89; Book 4, 90–106; and Book 5, 107–150. Each book ends with a doxology. Could it be that this grouping was intended to parallel the five books of Moses, the Torah, the first five books of the Bible? Scholars debate that point.

Psalms 1 and 2 serve as an introduction to the whole Psalter. Psalm 1 sets the theme:

> The LORD watches over the way of the righteous,
>   but the way of the wicked will perish. (v. 6)

Psalm 2 establishes the universality of God.

> The kings of the earth set themselves,
>   and the rulers take counsel together,
>   against the LORD and his anointed. (v. 2)
> He who sits in the heavens laughs;
>   the LORD has them in derision (v. 4)
> Now therefore, O kings, be wise;
>   be warned, O rulers of the earth.
> Serve the LORD with fear,
>   with trembling, kiss his feet. (vv. 10–12)

Psalm 150 concludes the Psalter with a doxology:

> Let everything that breathes praise the LORD!
> Praise the LORD!

Between these bookend themes, the universality of a righteous God and unbounded praise, arc to be found prayers and hymns that cover the whole range of human experience.

Using the Psalms Devotionally

Writing to his parents from a Gestapo prison, Dietrich Bonhoeffer said, "I am reading the Psalms daily, as I have done for years. I know them and love them more than any other book in the Bible."[1] A Christian minister, imprisoned for his opposition to the Nazi regime and eventually executed, found comfort and hope in these ancient songs of Israel.

When we pray the psalms, we join those across the centuries in monastery and hermitage, in church and home, in good times and terrible times, in prison and hospital, in war and peace, in synagogue and temple, who have also prayed them. We never pray them alone. Anytime we use

---

[1]Dietrich Bonhoeffer, *Prisoner for God: Letters and Papers from Prison* (New York: Macmillan, 1953), 33.

the psalms as our prayers, we can be sure that countless others around the world, at the same time, are also praying them.

Why has this spiritual practice endured? Why do these ancient songs, many born in a rural nomadic culture and referring to tents and flocks and herds, speak so powerfully to people in the twenty-first century? How is it that people find comfort in psalms that speak of vengeance, anger, and hostility? How can psalms that praise absolute monarchs speak to us in a democratic society?

We must not be put off by their antiquity, for they mirror universal human experiences. There is nothing time-bound in the search for God, in the reality of evil, in human selfishness. Such are found in every age and culture.

One of the difficulties many people have with prayer is setting the agenda. What do I pray about today? How can I avoid an endless repetition of the same things? What should I be praying about that I am neglecting? How can I move beyond just praying about my own selfish interests?

One solution is to let the Psalter set the agenda for you. While it is true that each of us has our own special concerns, the psalms cover the whole range of human experience. If we pray the psalms, most of what we would ever want to pray about will be covered.

Are you angry? There are many psalms you can pray on that subject. Do you feel neglected; do you think everyone is against you; have you been betrayed? There are psalms that cover all those problems. Are you frustrated because it seems that God has not done anything, has not heard your prayers, and has completely forsaken you? The psalms are full of that kind of language.

Do you have a deep longing for God, a desire to experience God's presence, a yearning to know God as it seems that people in Bible times did? So did the psalmists, and they expressed it often in the Psalter. Are you disappointed by the apparent silence of God? So were some of the psalmists. Are you moved to prayers of praise and thanksgiving to God? The psalms can help you pray them.

Some of the psalms can easily become our prayers. They express what we want to pray to God, and we can use their language. Others, however, are very difficult to pray, especially those that express violence, revenge, and hatred. There is a temptation to pass over or ignore the difficult psalms, such as psalm 109, but we must not do it. They are painful because they force us to face the same attitudes in ourselves and to deal with them. In this book I will attempt to show how we can pray all types of psalms. I cannot cover every psalm in the Psalter, but I will look at some representative samples. My hope is that when you read a verse I have quoted that strikes a responsive chord, you will be moved to read the entire psalm.

Walter Brueggemann, in his book *Praying the Psalms*, says that our efforts to pray the psalms are based on two things: what we bring to the psalms from our own lives and what we find when we come to the psalms.[2] We cannot separate our prayers from who we are. Authentic prayer takes into account both the good and the bad in us.

A friend once said to me that most of the Bible is God's word to us; the psalms are our words to God. They may not always be what God wants to hear from us, but in the best prayers, we offer to God who we are and pray for transformation. In his book *Praying the Psalms* Thomas Merton says, "In the last analysis, it is not so much what we get out of the psalms that rewards us, as what we put into them."[3]

---

[2]Walter Brueggemann, *Praying the Psalms* (Winona, Minn.: Saint Mary's Press, 1982), 27.

[3]Thomas Merton, *Praying the Psalms* (Collegeville, Minn.: The Liturgical Press, 1956), 45.

No serious prayer life can happen without considerable self-discipline. Each person has to work out a discipline for himself or herself. One valuable prayer discipline is praying psalms on a daily basis. How many depends on who you are. Some people may pray many, five or ten a day or more. Others would do well to pray one. Many classical spiritual writers warn against overdoing prayer. Don't commit yourself to doing more than is realistic. Prayer is not easy, and it should not be a source of overwhelming frustration.

Those who use breviaries—books that arrange the psalms for different times of the day—pray morning, noon, and night. Others feel fortunate if they can pray a psalm once a day. Some are morning people who want to begin the day with prayer. Others are night people who like to pray in the quiet of the evening when the day's work is done.

Some keep journals, writing down verses that happen to speak to them on a particular day, or writing out reflections on the experience of praying a given psalm. I would suggest that you begin simply, modestly. You can always expand what you do. The important thing is to open yourself to God. Praying the psalms over a period of days and months and years can have a profound effect. You may not have an instant insight or sudden dramatic change, but as the psalms become more familiar and their language becomes part of your own prayer, you may be formed over time into a very different person. That sense of God's presence may become clearer; your values may change; and, as Christians have throughout the ages, you may find a new intimacy with God.

The ultimate purpose of our prayer lives is to do what is expressed in Psalm 34:

O taste and see that the LORD is good. (v. 8)

So let us begin.

Longing for God

Maria had grown up in the church. Her parents took her to Sunday school and worship every Sunday. She took a hiatus from church during college, but she soon returned. The church habit had been so deeply ingrained in her that regular attendance seemed the normal, comfortable thing to do.

However, as she matured, she began to think more deeply about what church was actually all about. She found herself alienated by petty squabbles in the congregation, though she knew that such things occurred in every church. Committee meetings and covered dish dinners bored her. Many people, she discovered, were active because they needed a community. The fellowship of the congregation was what really drew them there.

While that was a nice bonus, Maria looked for something deeper. She wanted to know if there really was a God. Were the ideas the minister preached about every Sunday really true? Did God really care about individuals? Was it possible to have real contact with God? She had a longing for God that was more than just a philosophical curiosity. So much of her life had been invested in religious faith, but she had troubling doubts. Could she actually pray to a God about whom she was not sure? She wanted to develop a strong relationship with God, but when she prayed about it, God seemed strangely silent. The simple piety of her childhood faith was no longer enough.

The psalmists struggled with the same issues. Many of the psalms express a strong longing for God, a desire for God that seems unfulfilled. Yet the psalmists were drawn to the mystery of God and, in spite of their doubts, could praise God.

Their prayers could be Maria's prayers. They can be the prayers of any of us who are searching for God, yet still struggle with uncertainty. Psalm 42 gives us the language for appropriate prayer.

> As a deer longs for flowing streams,
>   so my soul longs for you, O God.
> My soul thirsts for God,
>   for the living God.
> When shall I come and behold
>   the face of God?
> My tears have been my food
>   day and night,
> while people say to me continually,
>   "Where is your God?" (vv. 1–3)

Maria had that thirst for God. She wanted to know when she would see the face of God, when she would know that divine presence. And when people asked her, "Where is your God?" she wanted to be able to answer confidently. The first verses of Psalm 42 were her prayer, a prayer that God, in a sense, had given her to pray.

The writer of Psalm 25 wrote, "For you I wait all day long" (v. 5), and Psalm 130 expresses the waiting that all religious people do:

> My soul waits for the Lord,
>> more than those who watch for the morning,
>> more than those who watch for the morning. (v. 6)

So Maria joined with the psalmist and all those who have prayed Psalm 61 over the centuries:

> Hear my cry, O God;
>> listen to my prayer.
> From the end of the earth I call to you,
>> when my heart is faint. (vv. 1–2)

Some people believe that the reason they have trouble finding God is that somehow God is angry with them. Many of the psalmists worried about that:

> O LORD, do not rebuke me in your anger
>> or discipline me in your wrath.
> Be gracious to me, O LORD, for I am languishing:
>> O LORD, heal me, for my bones are shaking with
>> terror.
> My soul also is struck with terror,
>> while you, O LORD—how long? (Ps. 6:1–3)

Sometimes people attribute bad things that happen to them to God's anger. Psalm 60 expresses that view:

> O God, you have rejected us, broken our defenses;
>> you have been angry; now restore us!

You have caused the land to quake; you have torn it
　　open;
　　repair the cracks in it, for it is tottering.
You have made your people suffer hard things. (vv. 1–3)

When things do not go for us as we wish they would,
we may be tempted to think that God is angry with us.
The reality may be that disobedience of moral law brings
pain into our lives because we have not acted responsibly.
If we have been unfaithful to our spouses or families,
the rejection of others is not caused by God, but by our
own stupidity. If we have gossiped or lied about another
person, it is not God's fault that people turn away from
us or criticize us. If we have been fundamentally dis-
honest and no one trusts us anymore, it is not God's
fault. It is because of our own behavior.

Of course God is angry over human sin and disobedience. Yet the obstacle to knowing God is not placed
there by God, but by us. By praying these psalms that seem
to express God's rejection, we are forced to look at ourselves
and see if there are reasons for the misfortunes that we are
so ready to blame on God.

The writer of Psalm 88 is ready to blame God for broken
relationships:

You have caused my companions to shun me;
　　you have made me a thing of horror to them.
I am shut in so that I cannot escape;
　　my eyes grow dim through sorrow. (vv. 8–9)
O LORD, why do you cast me off?
　　Why do you hide your face from me? (v. 14)

Blaming God for our troubles will always make it more
difficult to find God's presence in our lives. We should see
these psalms as a source of questions to raise about our

lives. What might we have done, for instance, that has caused others to reject us?

Another obstacle to our experience of God is a complaint that God does not do enough to defeat evil. Psalm 10 begins with a complaint:

> Why, O LORD, do you stand far off?
>> Why do you hide yourself in times of trouble?
> In arrogance the wicked persecute the poor—
>> let them be caught in the schemes they have
>>> devised. (vv. 1–2)

There follows a long account of the wicked, who act as if God does not pay any attention to them. But the psalm concludes on a positive note:

> But you do see! Indeed you note trouble and grief,
>> that you may take it into your hands...
> O LORD, you will hear the desire of the meek;
>> you will strengthen their heart, you will incline
>>> your ear
> to do justice for the orphan and the oppressed,
>> so that those from earth may strike terror no
>>> more. (vv. 14–18)

The search for God requires faith that God will be found. The psalmist realized that. While the tendency was to blame God for not addressing evil, the psalmist realized that God does indeed see evil in human experience and does not ignore it.

A similar development is described in Psalm 77. It begins with the usual lament that God is not doing anything:

> In the day of my trouble I seek the Lord;
>> in the night my hand is stretched out without
>>> wearying;

my soul refuses to be comforted.
I think of God, and I moan;
    I meditate, and my spirit faints. (vv. 2–3)
"Will the Lord spurn forever,
    and never again be favorable?
Has his steadfast love ceased forever?
    Are his promises at an end for all time?
Has God forgotten to be gracious?
    Has he in his anger shut up his compassion?"
    (vv. 7–9)

But then the psalmist reflects on what God has already done, and concludes the psalm by affirming the goodness of God:

I will call to mind the deeds of the LORD;
    I will remember your wonders of old.
I will meditate on all your work,
    and muse on your mighty deeds.
Your way, O God, is holy.
    What god is so great as our God?
You are the God who works wonders;
    you have displayed your might among the
        peoples. (vv. 11–14)

The memory of all that God has done in the past overcomes the frustration of not sensing that God was already present. Likewise, we must from time to time ponder all the good things that have happened to us that were not of our own making: friendships that suddenly developed, unexpected signs of love, an opportunity that we did not expect. The fact that we are even moved to pray at all is a sign that God is drawing us, reaching out to us, calling us.

Many of us spend time waiting for God. We wait for God to act. We wait for God to heal the sick person we love. We wait for God to defeat evil. We wait for God's self-revelation. We wait for God to come into our lives and our experiences. Psalm 40 says, "I waited patiently for the LORD; he inclined to me and heard my cry" (v. 1). Psalm 62 adds, "For God alone my soul waits in silence; from him comes my salvation" (v. 1). Psalm 59: "O my strength, I will watch for you; for you, O God, are my fortress" (v. 9).

The psalms give us excellent guidance for our search for God. They give us the language for expressing our longing for God. They warn us about the obstacles we can put in our way: assuming God is angry with us, complaining that God doesn't do what we want done about evil, being unwilling to wait for God.

Yet many of the psalmists affirm that waiting in silence, waiting patiently, and watching for signs of God's presence can lead us to the One for whom we search, the One whom Maria so earnestly sought.

Living with Frustration

John was a man who had great pride in his high standards for living. He took moral issues very seriously and was constantly upset when others did not measure up to what he thought was right. Some of his employees lived together without being married. Others refused to save any money, but spent their resources on lottery tickets and too much alcohol. He resented government welfare programs, complaining that people just did not want to work. He was especially bothered by political corruption, excessive government taxation and spending, and liberals, whom he thought were weakening the country. He believed that laziness on the part of his workers kept his business from reaching its full potential. In addition, his wife had some major health problems, his children often disappointed him, and his church would not take him seriously enough.

John needed to pray, but with so many frustrations in his life, prayer just didn't seem too relevant. What he needed to do, he believed, was tell people how they ought to live. He was an angry man: angry at other people, angry that the world was not what he thought it should be, angry that he could not control situations he believed needed change, angry at life in general. His minister tried to talk to him about his anger, but John thought that his minister was one of those naïve liberals who didn't live in the real world.

Prayer could change John's life if he would take it seriously. Many of the psalmists felt just as John did, and sharing that anger with God helped them deal with it.

Psalm 37 would be a good psalm for John to pray regularly. It instructs us to get rid of our anger at others.

> Do not fret because of the wicked;
>   do not be envious of wrongdoers,
> for they will soon fade like the grass,
>   and wither like the green herb. (vv. 1–2)
> Refrain from anger, and forsake wrath.
>   Do not fret—it only leads to evil. (v. 8)

The psalm promises that the wicked will not prevail forever.

> Yet a little while, and the wicked will be no more;
>   though you look diligently for their place, they
>   will not be there. (v. 10)

The psalmist counsels patience.

> Be still before the LORD, and wait patiently for him;
>   do not fret over those who prosper in their way,
>   over those who carry out evil devices. (v. 7)

Maintaining high values is worth the struggle, for the promise of the gospel is that evil will not finally win.

> I have seen the wicked oppressing,
>   and towering like a cedar of Lebanon.
> Again I passed by, and they were no more;
>   though I sought them, they could not be found.
> Mark the blameless, and behold the upright,
>   for there is posterity for the peaceable. (vv. 35–37)
> The salvation of the righteous is from the LORD;
>   he is their refuge in time of trouble. (v. 39)

How does John pray this psalm? He follows the psalmist's instruction and, first, prays that his anger can be overcome and that it will not lead him into evil. His constant criticism of everyone and everything will alienate him from other people, and that will only compound his frustration. So he prays for that patient stillness before God in the hope that this will enable him to see reality in a new perspective. He also prays in the hope that the evil he sees in the world will not last, but that God will finally prevail over it.

One of the best psalms for John to pray is Psalm 73. While we often worry about why good people suffer, this psalm is concerned with the question of why evil people prosper. The psalmist begins with an assumption many people make.

> Truly God is good to the upright,
>   to those who are pure in heart. (v. 1)

Many folks live in the belief that if they live good lives, God will take care of them. But then the psalmist raises the question of why people who have no religion, no morals, and no values seem to prosper, and the world loves them. The writer of Psalm 73 confesses,

> I was envious of the arrogant;
>> I saw the prosperity of the wicked. (v. 3)

We are then given a description of the wicked:

> They have no pain;
>> their bodies are sound and sleek.
> They are not in trouble as others are;
>> they are not plagued like other people.
> Therefore pride is their necklace;
>> violence covers them like a garment.
> Their eyes swell out with fatness;
>> their eyes overflow with follies.
> They scoff and speak with malice;
>> loftily they threaten oppression.
> They set their mouths against heaven,
>> and their tongues range over the earth. (vv. 4–9)
> Such are the wicked;
>> always at ease, they increase in riches. (v. 12)

But here is what really frustrates the psalmist:

> Therefore the people turn and praise them,
>> and find no fault in them. (v. 10)

So the psalmist questions whether trying to live a virtuous life has been worthwhile.

> All in vain I have kept my heart clean
>> and washed my hands in innocence. (v. 13)

No doubt John feels that way from time to time. Is it really worth it to try to do the right thing when people without religious values seem to be so successful?

> But when I thought how to understand this,
>> it seemed to me a wearisome task. (v. 16)

Indeed, it is a wearisome task. People who live wonderful lives of virtue and high morality often suffer, and those with little moral sensitivity are often hugely successful. The psalmist confesses frustration:

> When my soul was embittered,
>   when I was pricked in heart,
> I was stupid and ignorant. (vv. 21–22)

But now there is a recognition that in the midst of frustration, God is still present.

> Nevertheless I am continually with you;
>   you hold my right hand.
> You guide me with your counsel,
>   and afterward you will receive me with honor.
> Whom have I in heaven but you?
>   And there is nothing on earth that I desire other
>   than you.
> My flesh and my heart may fail,
>   but God is the strength of my heart and my
>   portion forever. (vv. 23–26)

The best way to deal with frustration is to deepen one's intimacy with God. Psalm 73 is one that many people can pray. It is an offering to God of all our complaints and frustration, and a recognition that if we maintain our relationship with God, we will see all our issues in perspective. Others may not behave as we would like, but God still holds us by the right hand. There is nothing we need more than that.

Psalm 112 takes another approach to the question of frustration. It praises those "who fear the LORD, who greatly delight in his commandments" (v. 1). Here the key to dealing with the reality of the wicked is to be just and generous.

It is well with those who deal generously and lend,
    who conduct their affairs with justice.
For the righteous will never be moved;
    they will be remembered forever.
They are not afraid of evil tidings;
    their hearts are firm, secure in the LORD.
Their hearts are steady, they will not be afraid. (vv. 5–8)

Such folks are outgoing and giving people.

They have distributed freely, they have given to the
        poor;
    their righteousness endures forever. (v. 9)

Such generosity and righteousness have a powerful impact
on the wicked.

The wicked see it and are angry;
    they gnash their teeth and melt away;
    the desire of the wicked comes to nothing. (v. 10)

What will help John to overcome his frustrations is to
become a more loving, caring, and compassionate person.
His constant anger will never solve any problem. It may
even endanger his health. Psalm 112 leads us to pray that
we may become more just, generous, and caring people. It
will be difficult to open ourselves to God if we cannot be
open to other people. Certainly the gospel teaches us that
one way to face down evil is to be more loving. It may not
stop evil from taking place, but it will enable us to deal
with it more fruitfully.

Still, there are many psalms of frustration with which
we can easily identify. It is difficult to maintain faith when
God seems to be hidden from us. Psalm 44 says:

Why do you hide your face?
    Why do you forget our affliction and oppression?
        (v. 24)

Psalm 43 raises the same question:

> For you are the God in whom I take refuge;
>> why have you cast me off? (v. 2)

If we need the language to express our frustrations to God, these psalms provide it for us. Psalm 102 is another psalm of pain and frustration:

> For my days pass away like smoke,
>> and my bones burn like a furnace.
> My heart is stricken and withered like grass;
>> I am too wasted to eat my bread. (vv. 3–4)
> I lie awake;
>> I am like a lonely bird on the housetop. (v. 7)

This sounds like an illness. If it is, it is because of what is happening to the psalmist.

> All day long my enemies taunt me;
>> those who deride me use my name for a curse. (v. 8)

The psalmist blames God for these troubles.

> Because of your indignation and anger;
>> for you have lifted me up and thrown me aside.
>> (v. 10)
> He [God] has broken my strength in midcourse;
>> he has shortened my days. (v. 23)

Did God cause these troubles, or was some moral law violated, and suffering resulted? Why have his enemies taunted him?

When we experience suffering in our lives, we naturally ask, Why is this happening to us? Is this God's punishment for something we have done or something we are? When we feel this way, we can identify with this psalm. There may well be times when we think that God has lifted us up and thrown us aside.

Whether that is truly the case or not, this psalmist can still affirm the sovereignty of God and can declare God's goodness.

> But you, O LORD, are enthroned forever;
>   your name endures to all generations. (v. 12)
> For the LORD will build up Zion;
>   he will appear in his glory. (v. 16)

The psalmist's prayer is a strong belief in the eternal God:

> Long ago you laid the foundation of the earth,
>   and the heavens are the work of your hands.
> They will perish, but you endure;
>   they will all wear out like a garment.
> You change them like clothing, and they pass away;
>   but you are the same, and your years have no end.
>   (vv. 25–27)

We may pray this prayer in the misery of a situation which may or may not be of our own making, and we may want to ask God if there is a reason for it that we cannot see. It may well be that we know we have displeased God in some way, and this psalm becomes an appropriate prayer for us. But at the same time, we pray the affirmation that

> He [God] will regard the prayer of the destitute,
>   and will not despise their prayer. (v. 17)

The One who will hear us is the eternal God who created everything and who endures forever. It is not always possible to bring good out of evil, to remedy situations that we know are not right. Psalm 120 is a prayer with which we may well identify.

> Too long have I had my dwelling
>   among those who hate peace.

I am for peace,
   but when I speak, they are for war. (vv. 6–7)

The psalms clearly recognize human frustration. They give us the language to express it to God. They also give us the affirmation that God is still in control. We cannot fix everything, but we can live in intimacy with God, who puts our complaints in perspective and who helps us understand what is most important about our lives. In the light of the grand scheme of eternity, many of our worries lose their force.

Psalm 80 asks,

How long will you be angry with your people's
   prayers? (v. 4)

Interestingly enough, it has a refrain that is used three times in the psalm. It is a good refrain to be used in all our prayers.

Restore us, O LORD God of hosts;
   let your face shine, that we may be saved. (v. 19)

Finding the Gospel in the Psalms

Cindy grew up in a very strict home. Her parents attended a church that attempted to motivate the congregation with guilt. Sermon after sermon emphasized that God is not pleased with people who misbehave, who have moral lapses. No matter how hard she tried, her parents were always telling her that her behavior was not going to please God. She grew up with a terrible fear of the judgment of God, knowing that she was not good enough to avoid condemnation.

Even her most minor lapses usually resulted in some kind of punishment. On more than one occasion she was sent to bed without her dinner. She was often prevented from going places with friends. She dreaded her parents' harsh words of criticism. She wanted to be a good person, but it seemed that she was never good enough. For her, Jesus was the one who will judge us at the last day, and she never saw him as a loving redeemer who forgives and shows mercy.

She didn't know what to pray. How does one pray to a God who inspires only fear, dread, and judgment? What does one say to a God whose eyes search out the most minor infraction? Cindy had been raised in the church and had been taught that it was important to the state of her soul, but she never saw the church as a place of joy and peace.

What Cindy needed was a new understanding of the Christian gospel. She needed to know that God is a God of love and mercy, that Jesus' ministry was spent caring for marginalized people whom the rest of society tended to condemn.

Most, and perhaps all, the psalms were composed before the time of Jesus. If we take a linear view of history, it would seem that there is no way that the Christian gospel could be expressed in them. But the gospel is a timeless message of God's mercy and forgiveness, and we can find it expressed in many places in the psalms.

One of the most obvious places is Psalm 130. It begins with a cry asking that God listen to us:

> Out of the depths I cry to you, O Lord.
>   Lord, hear my voice!
> Let your ears be attentive
>   to the voice of my supplications! (vv. 1–2)

Loose translation: God, listen to me! The next verses, however, are ones that Cindy should ponder, for they express the essence of the gospel:

> If you, O Lord, should mark iniquities,
>   Lord, who could stand?

> But there is forgiveness with you,
>> so that you may be revered. (vv. 3–4)

That is the good news for Cindy. God does not hold our iniquities against us. If that were the case, we would all be doomed. The gospel promise is the promise of forgiveness:

> For with the LORD there is steadfast love,
>> and with him is great power to redeem. (v. 7)

If Cindy could come to understand that, she could pray prayers of praise and thanksgiving, knowing that the harsh judgment of her parents and her church is not what God has to offer. Rather, God offers us forgiveness and redemption. So we cry to God out of our depths, knowing that the One we want to hear us treats us with steadfast love. That is what Jesus came to teach us.

We often find gospel affirmations in strange places in the psalms. Psalm 68 speaks of battle, captives, shattering the heads of enemies, the spoils of war, and bloodshed. Yet in the midst of that we find words of the gospel:

> Blessed be the Lord
>> who daily bears us up.
>> God is our salvation.
> Our God is a God of salvation,
>> and to GOD, the Lord,
>>> belongs escape from death. (vv. 19–20)

Some may say that this is taking a passage out of context. However, the imagery of the gospel is so strong here that we cannot fail to notice it. In the midst of expressions of human strife comes a divine word: God daily bears us up and is the source of our salvation. Ancient Israel heard that in the context of war. We hear it in the context of our own struggles with evil. The psalm concludes:

> Awesome is God in his sanctuary,
>> the God of Israel;
>> he gives power and strength to his people. (v. 35)

Psalm 81, another expression of God's mercy, begins with Israel's praise.

> Sing aloud to God our strength;
>> shout for joy to the God of Jacob. (v. 1)

This psalm is written as a dialogue between Israel and God. While Israel praises, God complains:

> "But my people did not listen to my voice;
>> Israel would not submit to me." (v. 11)
> "O that my people would listen to me,
>> that Israel would walk in my ways!" (v. 13)

But God promises good things to those who will listen, who will give themselves to God. Reminding people that divine power had brought them out of Egypt, God said,

> "Open your mouth wide and I will fill it." (v. 10)

God promises to nourish us in faith.

> "I would feed you with the finest of the wheat,
>> and with honey from the rock I would satisfy
>> you." (v. 16)

As Christians, we cannot help but think of the finest wheat as the bread of heaven, that bread that represents the broken body of Christ, that eucharistic bread that promises us the blessings of the gospel. Of course, this is not what the author of this psalm had in mind, but the image is there, and for those of us who are fed regularly at the table of the Lord, we are once again reminded of the gospel promises. There are so many images in the psalms that bring the gospel to our minds. When we are sensitive to them, the psalms can take on new meaning. They are no longer just the praises or laments of Israel for us, but they stimulate our awareness of what Christ has promised.

In this regard, Psalm 103 is a classic. It begins with a profound statement of praise:

> Bless the LORD, O my soul,
>> and all that is within me,
>> bless his holy name. (v. 1)

There are some wonderful gospel passages in this psalm:

> Bless the LORD, O my soul,
>> and do not forget all his benefits—
> who forgives all your iniquity,
>> who heals all your diseases,
> who redeems your life from the Pit,
>> who crowns you with steadfast love and mercy.
>> (vv. 2–4)

The psalmist expresses the faith that God understands our human condition.

> The LORD is merciful and gracious,
>> slow to anger and abounding in steadfast love.
> He will not always accuse,
>> nor will he keep his anger forever.
> He does not deal with us according to our sins,
>> nor repay us according to our iniquities.
> For as the heavens are high above the earth,
>> so great is his steadfast love toward those who fear
>>> him;
> as far as the east is from the west,
>> so far he removes our transgressions from us.

As a father has compassion for his children,
    so the LORD has compassion for those who fear
    him.
For he knows how we were made;
    he remembers that we are dust. (vv. 8–14)

Those are words that Cindy needs to understand, and they should enable her to pray, "Bless the LORD, O my soul, and all that is within me bless his holy name."

Once again we have seen the basics of the gospel expressed in an ancient psalm of Israel. God does not deal with us according to our sins, but according to steadfast love. So we are stimulated to offer prayers of praise and thanksgiving that God deals with us as a parent who has compassion for its children.

Book 5 of the Psalter opens with Psalm 107, a remarkable account of the cycle of the relationship of God's way with us. It has an introduction, four accounts of God's redemptive activity, and a conclusion.

The introduction is an admonition to be thankful.

O give thanks to the LORD, for he is good;
    for his steadfast love endures forever.
Let the redeemed of the LORD say so,
    those he redeemed from trouble. (vv. 1–2)

Accounts of trouble, repentance, and salvation follow. The first is about people who wandered in desert wastes, lost, hungry, and thirsty:

They cried to the LORD in their trouble [repentance],
    and he delivered them from their distress
    [salvation];
he led them by a straight way,
    until they reached an inhabited town. (vv. 6–7)

The account closes with thanksgiving:

> Let them thank the LORD for his steadfast love,
>   for his wonderful works to humankind. (v. 8)

This verse is repeated at the end of each of the four accounts. Then there is a verse specific to the situation that has been described:

> For he satisfies the thirsty,
>   and the hungry he fills with good things. (v. 9)

The second account deals with prisoners "in misery and in irons," who had rebelled against God:

> Their hearts were bowed down with hard labor;
>   they fell down, with no one to help.
> Then they cried to the LORD in their trouble,
>   and he saved them from their distress;
> he brought them out of darkness and gloom,
>   and broke their bonds asunder. (vv. 12–14)

The repetitive thanksgiving line appears again, followed by the specific reference:

> Let them thank the LORD for his steadfast love,
>   for his wonderful works to humankind.
> For he shatters the doors of bronze,
>   and cuts in two the bars of iron. (vv. 15–16)

The third account is about those who "were sick through their sinful ways and because of their iniquities endured affliction" (v. 17). The fourth describes those who "went down to the sea in ships" (v. 23) and encountered violent storms. In each case the people cried to God, and God saved them. What is described here is the cycle of the human condition and the mercy of God. People have troubles; they turn to God; and God delivers them. In two of the accounts people had brought their misery upon themselves by ignoring God. But repentance brought salvation.

The rest of the psalm describes both the power and the mercy of God. God can turn rivers into deserts and parched lands into pools of water.

> When they are diminished and brought low
>   through oppression, trouble, and sorrow,
> he pours contempt on princes…
> but he raises up the needy out of distress,
>   and makes their families like flocks. (vv. 39–41)

Cindy was taught that repentance is never good enough to ensure salvation. She never felt deserving of God's forgiveness. This psalm stimulates our turning to God in the faith that God hears us when we know our lives have not been what they should be. Recognizing our disobedience, our neglect of God, our hostile attitudes, and our misdirected values turns us toward God and the gospel promise of God's mercy. So we thank God for that steadfast love and those wonderful works to humankind.

The most important factor in developing a deep relationship with God is not the way we pray or how we meditate or even the sacrificial way we may live. The most important factor is developing a contemplative attitude, an attitude that is sensitive to God's presence and what God is doing. Praying the psalms helps develop that attitude. As we read these songs of praise and thanksgiving for what God had done in ancient Israel, we may become more sensitive to what God is doing in our lives and our communities. Look for God's presence in the ordinary events of your life, and you will be able to pray with enthusiasm the final doxology of Psalm 72:

Blessed be the LORD, the God of Israel,
    who alone does wondrous things.
Blessed be his glorious name forever;
    may his glory fill the whole earth.
    Amen and Amen. (vv. 18–19)

Religious Experience

Todd heard his friends talk about their religion. Some seemed to him to be a little too aggressive, yet he was interested in what they had to say. They talked about their conversations with God and their companionship with Jesus. They would often say things like, "I asked God what to do and God said…"

He wondered, *Is it really possible to know God?* These people seemed so sure of their faith. Todd was a seeker. He had a feeling that there really was something to religion, but he had never heard God's voice speaking to him. He tried sitting in silence, listening for God, but nothing seemed to happen. He went to church and tried to worship. The music was nice; the atmosphere was peaceful and comforting; even the sermon was rather stimulating. People were friendly and made him feel at home. However, his quest for some kind of religious experience was rewarded with silence. Is all this talk about God, he wondered, really true? The psalmists believed that it was, and consequently many of the psalms recount the psalmists' religious experiences.

One of the most loved of all the psalms is Psalm 23. Children memorize it in Sunday school; it is often read at funerals; and if people know anything about the psalms at all, they know this one:

> The LORD is my shepherd, I shall not want.
>   He makes me lie down in green pastures;
> he leads me beside still waters;
>   he restores my soul.
> He leads me in right paths for his name's sake. (vv. 1–3)

The psalmist had a sense that God was present in his life, leading him in good directions.

> Even though I walk through the darkest valley,
>   I fear no evil;
> for you are with me. (v. 4)

There is no report of hearing voices, of being told what to do, but there is a deep sense of God's care and guidance. This psalmist was sensitive to the good things happening in his life and attributed them to God. He had that contemplative attitude that enabled him to see what God was doing in his life.

Todd might be helped if he would examine his own life experience, particularly those areas where good things happen, where love is expressed, where, through no effort of his own, things work out in positive ways. There are more ways to be guided by God than by hearing a divine voice speaking to you.

A similar idea is found at the end of Psalm 27. The psalm begins with a strong affirmation of faith.

The LORD is my light and my salvation;
  whom shall I fear?
The LORD is the stronghold of my life;
  of whom shall I be afraid? (v. 1)

The body of the psalm is a plea for God's help, but the conclusion is an expression of seeing God at work in the world.

I believe that I shall see the goodness of the LORD
  in the land of the living.
Wait for the LORD;
  be strong, and let your heart take courage;
  wait for the LORD. (vv. 13–14)

Psalm 46 also speaks of seeing God at work. It too begins with a strong affirmation of faith:

God is our refuge and strength,
  a very present help in trouble.
Therefore we will not fear, though the earth should
    change,
  though the mountains shake in the heart of the
    sea. (vv. 1–2)

At the end, the psalmist counsels looking at what God has done in the world:

Come, behold the works of the LORD;
  see what desolations he has brought on the earth.
He makes wars cease to the end of the earth;
  he breaks the bow, and shatters the spear;
  he burns the shields with fire. (vv. 8–9)

Then comes the admonition to listen:

> "Be still, and know that I am God!
>> I am exalted among the nations,
>> I am exalted in the earth."
> The LORD of hosts is with us;
>> the God of Jacob is our refuge. (vv. 10–11)

There is a certain stillness required of us if we would have insight into what God is doing in our lives and in the world. So many distractions keep us from seeing the divine action. Our minds are churning with input, and we are often overwhelmed with things we have to do. The psalm reminds us, "Be still, be still, be still." In that stillness we may find the God for whom we have been searching.

Psalm 131 gives us similar instruction. It calls for humility.

> O LORD, my heart is not lifted up,
>> my eyes are not raised too high;
> I do not occupy myself with things
>> too great and too marvelous for me. (v. 1)

This psalmist also wrote of stillness, but using a slightly different image.

> I have calmed and quieted my soul,
>> like a weaned child with its mother;
>> my soul is like the weaned child that is with me.
>> (v. 2)

One of the great classics of the Psalter is Psalm 139. It reflects a belief that God is always present in the psalmist's life, even in the womb:

> It was you who formed my inward parts;
>> you knit me together in my mother's womb…

> My frame was not hidden from you,
> when I was being made in secret,
>> intricately woven in the depths of the earth.
>>> (vv. 13–15)

Psalm 139 begins with a statement on God's knowledge of us:

> O LORD, you have searched me and known me.
> You know when I sit down and when I rise up;
>> you discern my thoughts from far away.
> You search out my path and my lying down,
>> and are acquainted with all my ways.
> Even before a word is on my tongue,
>> O LORD, you know it completely. (vv. 1–4)

Although the psalmist affirms such a presence, it is hard to understand:

> Such knowledge is too wonderful for me;
>> it is so high that I cannot attain it. (v. 6)

Not only does the psalmist affirm God's constant presence, but the reality is that one is never away from it:

> Where can I go from your spirit?
>> Or where can I flee from your presence?
> If I ascend to heaven, you are there;
>> if I make my bed in Sheol, you are there. (vv. 7–8)

One of the great religious classics of the twentieth century is Dag Hammarskjold's journal, *Markings*. Hammarskjold was the Secretary-General of the United Nations from 1953 until his death in 1962. During a flight to China to attempt to secure the release of American airmen, he entered into his journal the next lines from Psalm 139:

If I take the wings of the morning
    and settle at the farthest limits of the sea,
even there your hand shall lead me,
    and your right hand hold me fast.[1]

This psalm is a prayer that acknowledges God's presence. Todd might ponder this psalm and offer it as his own prayer. There is a sense that before one can have a deep relationship with God, one must be overwhelmed by the awesomeness of God.

How weighty to me are your thoughts, O God!
    How vast is the sum of them!
I try to count them—they are more than the sand;
    I come to the end—I am still with you.
        (vv. 17–18)

The greatness, omnipotence, and holiness of God may be more than we can understand, but for the psalmists these things do not make contact with God impossible—"I am still with you."

The last section of the psalm is difficult for many people. There are sentiments expressed that would seem contrary to the Christian ethic.

O that you would kill the wicked, O God,
    and that the bloodthirsty would depart from
        me...
Do I not hate those who hate you, O LORD?
    And do I not loathe those who rise up against
        you?
I hate them with perfect hatred;
    I count them my enemies. (vv. 19–22)

[1]Henry P. Van Dusen, *Dag Hammarskjold: The Statesman and His Faith* (New York: Harper and Row, 1964), 131.

Difficult psalms are discussed in chapter 7. However, for now may I suggest that the hated enemy in this psalm is not other people, but those forces that keep us from knowing God. We wrestle with many interior demons: anger, prejudice, jealousy, fear, hostility toward others, temptation. We could name many others. These hated enemies torment us all the time. Would that God would destroy them so that we could reach our full potential as children of God and know that we live with a Divine Presence.

Those who hope to hear a voice from heaven should meditate on Psalm 19:

> There is no speech, nor are there words,
>   their voice is not heard;
> yet their voice goes out through all the earth,
>   and their words to the end of the world. (vv. 3–4)

These are voices that are not audible to the human ear, yet are very clear. The voice of God is known in many ways: nature, art, music, human interaction, compassionate love, the normal events of daily life, and the big events of history. The most important factor in our quest for God is not the way we pray. Rather, it is the development of a contemplative attitude, a sensitivity to the presence of God in our midst. It involves expectant listening as opposed to giving God orders. It is not a sensitivity that can be developed overnight, but praying the psalms can help to foster and develop a listening heart.

6

Confessing Sins with the Psalms

Susan's life had not gone as she had wanted it to go. She grew up in a middle-class, middle America home. Her parents were good, churchgoing people. Her father had a decent job that provided an adequate income, and her mother stayed at home to help raise Susan, her younger brother, and her older sister. Friends looked on them as a rather ideal American family.

In her teenage years Susan began to rebel. She resented having to go to church; she felt stifled by her parents' moderate conservatism; and she believed that there was another lifestyle out there that would be more exciting than what she experienced at home. Like many of her generation she began to experiment with drugs and became sexually active, and her frustrated parents found her to be uncontrollable.

When she barely graduated from high school, she refused to go to college. Instead, she took a low-wage job at a discount store and moved in with friends who were determined to test their newfound freedoms to the limit.

It took several years for Susan to realize that her life was going nowhere. All she could see ahead of her was living on the edge of poverty with people who only wanted to be high on drugs and engage in meaningless sex. When she discovered she was pregnant, she realized that something had to change in her life. She hated having to tell her parents that she had made serious mistakes, but her friends were offering no help. Indeed, when they discovered she was pregnant, they began to abandon her. She was sure that her parents would tell her, "We told you so, but you wouldn't listen." Still, she needed a haven of love, and she knew that after the initial condemning confrontation her parents would provide that.

The baby was put up for adoption, and Susan enrolled in the local college. The reentry into academic life was difficult. Her grades had gone down in her last two years of high school because she refused to study. Developing academic discipline was not easy. Drugs had taken their toll, and she found it difficult to concentrate.

She signed up reluctantly for a required religion course. Because the college was church related everyone had to take it, but Susan postponed it as long as she could. She was surprised to discover that the course was not Sunday school, but a serious academic study of religion. She became intrigued with the questions that were raised and with new approaches, at least new to her, to thinking about faith matters. She began to see that the religious values of her parents, while they might have been a bit naïve, had substance to them that she had refused to face. She sought counseling from the college chaplain, who encouraged her to develop a faith of her own. She discovered that the campus Christian group was made up largely of students who had been raised in church but still had many questions. Long discussions in the student center coffee shop caused her to think more deeply about God and the need for a Christian community.

Now she began to wrestle with feelings of profound guilt. How could she face the God she had begun to discover? Was God going to condemn her for her past life? The memories of those days tormented her. Somehow she needed to put that behind her and begin anew, but how does one begin anew with all the baggage of irresponsibility that she carried?

Susan needed to confess, to unload her guilt, and become a new person. But how could she do that? Simply reciting the mistakes of her past to others did not seem to help.

She needed what the psalms had to offer: ways to confess sins and become transformed. There are a number of psalms that are specifically designed for such confession. If Susan were to study them and make them her prayers, she might find the help she needs.

Many of us, in so many words, pray the first lines of Psalm 6:

> O LORD, do not rebuke me in your anger,
>   or discipline me in your wrath. (v. 1)

But there is more to confession than fear. If done in light of the gospel, it becomes a positive experience.

Seven psalms in the Psalter have traditionally been regarded as penitential psalms, or psalms of confession: 6, 32, 38, 51, 102, 130, and 143.

Psalm 32 begins with a fundamental statement of the Christian gospel, an affirmation of forgiveness:

> Happy are those whose transgression is forgiven,
>   whose sin is covered.
> Happy are those to whom the LORD imputes no
>   iniquity,
>   and in whose spirit there is no deceit. (vv. 1–2)

The psalmist then describes the problem of not confessing:

> While I kept silence, my body wasted away
>   through my groaning all day long.
> For day and night your hand was heavy upon me;
>   my strength was dried up as by the heat of
>   summer. (vv. 3–4)

Guilt can take a heavy toll on us. It can affect us both emotionally and physically.

Finally, the psalmist decided to confess and, as a result, experienced forgiveness:

> Then I acknowledged my sin to you,
>   and I did not hide my iniquity.
> I said, "I will confess my transgressions to the LORD,"
>   and you forgave the guilt of my sin. (v. 5)

It was honest confession that brought a sense of forgiveness, a sense not experienced by keeping silence. So the psalmist encourages others to confess in like manner:

> Therefore let all who are faithful
>   offer prayer to you;
> at a time of distress, the rush of mighty waters
>   shall not reach them.
> You are a hiding place for me;
>   you preserve me from trouble;
>   you surround me with glad cries of deliverance.
>   (vv. 6–7)

The psalm concludes with a call to faith.

> Many are the torments of the wicked,
>> but steadfast love surrounds those who trust in
>> the LORD. (v. 10)

Susan was experiencing some of that torment, but she needed to understand the gospel promise of God's steadfast love. The psalmist experienced that after confessing.

The classic psalm of confession is Psalm 51. According to tradition, this was the psalm David prayed after he was caught in the affair with Bathsheba (2 Sam. 11, 12). It is a prayer that anyone who needs to find the words to confess sins could use:

> Have mercy on me, O God,
>> according to your steadfast love;
> according to your abundant mercy,
>> blot out my transgressions.
> Wash me thoroughly from my iniquity,
>> and cleanse me from my sin.
> For I know my transgressions,
>> and my sin is ever before me.
> Against you, you alone, have I sinned,
>> and done what is evil in your sight,
> so that you are justified in your sentence,
>> and blameless when you pass judgment. (vv. 1–4)

The next sentence is problematic for some people:

> Indeed, I was born guilty,
>> a sinner when my mother conceived me. (v. 5)

The idea of original sin may be difficult for some folks. Many psalms express the idea that we all have an inclination to evil. Human selfishness is what drives us. We all want what we want out of life, rather than what God may want from us. Many people find that doing good is an uphill battle, while taking the selfish way is easier. Susan certainly found that. The sins of some of us may be more subtle than hers: prejudice, a secret hatred, racism, being judgmental, ignoring human need, jealousy, unfaithfulness. We carry those emotions and feelings around with us. Most of the time we keep them repressed, but from time to time they rise to the surface and get out of control, and we find ourselves having said things and done things that we instantly regret. That is our human nature, and that makes regular confession an important spiritual discipline for us.

However, the Christian gospel does not call on us to feel guilty all the time. In his wonderful book *Whatever Became of Sin?* Karl Menninger tells of an incident that occurred on a street corner in the Chicago Loop in 1972. A stern-faced man pointed at people as they hurried across the intersection and shouted, "Guilty!" He repeated the gesture, pointed at people he did not know and said, "Guilty!" One person turned to another and asked, "But how did he know?"[1]

We all carry various degrees of guilt with us. But the gospel does not focus on that. It focuses on our becoming new people. So does Psalm 51:

Purge me with hyssop, and I shall be clean;
    wash me, and I shall be whiter than snow. (v. 7)
Hide your face from my sins,
    and blot out all my iniquities. (v. 9)

Every prayer of confession must be accompanied by a prayer for renewal, a prayer that we may become new people:

---

[1]Karl Menninger, *Whatever Became of Sin?* (New York: Hawthorn Books, 1973), 1–2.

Create in me a clean heart, O God,
  and put a new and right spirit within me.
Do not cast me away from your presence,
  and do not take your holy spirit from me.
Restore to me the joy of your salvation,
  and sustain me with a willing spirit. (vv. 10–12)

What does God require of us? The psalmist did not think that God really wanted burnt offerings. God wanted something much more important and transforming:

The sacrifice acceptable to God is a broken spirit;
  a broken and contrite heart, O God, you will not
    despise. (v. 17)

Susan had that. After confessing to God, her prayer now should be for a new and right spirit, a transformation into a new person, a transformation that has already begun, but can be assured by God's grace. This is a very complete psalm, as it includes all the elements of a good confession: contrition, confession, a prayer for transformation, and praise of God.

O Lord, open my lips,
  and my mouth will declare your praise. (v. 15)

Sometimes we are not aware of our sins because our culture blinds us to them. In some cultural contexts, racism and anti-Semitism, for example, may be considered normal attitudes. This kind of cultural conditioning is not always easy to transcend. In such situations we need to pray Psalm 19:

But who can detect their errors?
  Clear me from hidden faults. (v. 12)

Other psalms also have good language to use in confession:

O God, you know my folly;
   the wrongs I have done are not hidden from you.
     (69:5)
Help us, O God of our salvation,
   for the glory of your name;
deliver us, and forgive our sins,
   for your name's sake. (79:9)
LORD, you were favorable to your land;
   you restored the fortunes of Jacob.
You forgave the iniquity of your people;
   you pardoned all their sin.
You withdrew all your wrath;
   you turned from your hot anger.
Restore us again, O God of our salvation,
   and put away your indignation toward us. (85:1–4)

Susan will find no peace until she honestly opens herself to God and confesses her failures and irresponsible actions. Beyond that, she needs to confess that she gave in to human selfishness too easily. Having done that, she then needs to pray for renewal, that she may become the person God wants her to be and that God will give her the grace to grow in her faith and knowledge. She needs to understand the Christian gospel promise—that she is exactly the kind of person that Jesus reached out to and touched with a healing hand. As Jesus said at a dinner party in a tax collector's home, "'Those who are well have no need of a physician, but those who are sick; I have come to call not the righteous but sinners'" (Mk. 2:17).

Violence, Vengeance, Anger, and Judgment

John, who was mentioned in chapter 3 as a habitually angry person, might find too much comfort in some of the psalms. The ones presented in this chapter seem full of his self-righteous anger. The danger is that such selfish-righteousness can lead one to violence.

Many people are put off by the psalms because they find them too violent and too full of vengeance and other unhappy qualities. Those elements are certainly there:

> You strike all my enemies on the cheek;
>   you break the teeth of the wicked. (Ps. 3:7)

Psalm 58 is a prayer to destroy the wicked.

O God, break the teeth in their mouths;
>   tear out the fangs of the young lions, O LORD!
Let them vanish like water that runs away;
>   like grass let them be trodden down and wither.
Let them be like the snail that dissolves into slime;
>   like the untimely birth that never sees the sun.
>   (vv. 6–8)
The righteous will rejoice when they see vengeance
>   done;
>   they will bathe their feet in the blood of the
>   wicked. (v. 10)

Psalm 68 speaks of taking captives and the spoils of war, and adds:

God will shatter the heads of his enemies,
>   the hairy crown of those who walk in their guilty
>   ways. (v. 21)

Psalm 79 is a prayer for God's anger to be redirected:

Will you be angry forever?
>   Will your jealous wrath burn like fire?
Pour out your anger on the nations
>   that do not know you,
and on the kingdoms
>   that do not call on your name. (vv. 5–6)

Psalm 101 has a tone of John's self-righteousness about it. The psalmist speaks of the psalmist's own integrity, loyalty, and justice, but then moves to violence:

No one who practices deceit
>   shall remain in my house;
no one who utters lies
>   shall continue in my presence.

Morning by morning I will destroy
    all the wicked in the land,
cutting off all evildoers
from the city of the LORD. (vv. 7–8)

Much evil has been done in the world as an expression
of people's exalted view of their own righteousness.
Holocausts in Europe, Cambodia, Rwanda, Bosnia, and in
our own land of Native Americans and African Americans.
All have been carried out in the name of people's self-
righteousness, with a belief that they were destroying evil
people.

How can a Christian possibly pray psalms like Psalm 110?

The LORD is at your right hand;
    he will shatter kings on the day of his wrath.
He will execute judgment among the nations,
    filling them with corpses;
he will shatter heads
    over the wide earth. (vv. 5–6)

Similarly, the obvious context of Psalm 137 is the exile of
the people of Judah, whose nation has been destroyed by
Babylonia. It tells of people weeping "by the rivers of
Babylon" who found themselves unable to "sing the LORD's
song in a foreign land." Their anger is so intense that the
psalm proclaims:

O daughter Babylon, you devastator!
    Happy shall they be who pay you back
    what you have done to us!
Happy shall they be who take your little ones
    and dash them against the rock!
      (vv. 8–9)

Can we pray that?

One of the angriest psalms is Psalm 109, in which the psalmist has been grievously wronged by an enemy.

> Wicked and deceitful mouths are opened against me,
>   speaking against me with lying tongues.
> They beset me with words of hate,
>   and attack me without cause.
> In return for my love they accuse me,
>   even while I make prayer for them. (vv. 2–3)

The psalmist uses courtroom imagery against the enemy:

> "Appoint a wicked man against him;
>   let an accuser stand on his right.
> When he is tried, let him be found guilty;
>   let his prayer be counted as sin." (vv. 6–7)

There follows a catalog of terrible things that the psalmist wants done to the enemy:

> "May his days be few;
>   may another seize his position.
> May his children be orphans,
>   and his wife a widow.
> May his children wander about and beg;
>   may they be driven out of the ruins they inhabit.
> May the creditor seize all that he has;
>   may strangers plunder the fruits of his toil.
> May there be no one to do him a kindness,
>   nor anyone to pity his orphaned children." (vv. 8–12)

There is real anger! Something terrible must have been done to the writer of this psalm. How in the world can we pray this?

When we read this psalm we likely have two reactions. First, we are repulsed. We have been conditioned to think that a Christian should never wish evil on another person.

But second, if we are honest with ourselves, we realize that we have probably been that angry at some points in our lives.

One of the great things about the psalms is their humanity. They make us aware of who we really are. This psalm brings to the surface an awareness of our own anger. It opens up that side of ourselves that we usually keep repressed, but that occasionally gets out of control. It reminds us what anger can do to us and that we have to face it and do something about it. We all have demons that need to be cast out, demons that are often hidden and even unconscious, but that come out on occasion when our anger gets the best of us.

There is another way to look at this psalm, and that is to internalize it. We all carry around anger, prejudice, jealousy, envy, greed, unfaithfulness, and other problems. These are the demons that we want orphaned. These qualities produce offspring of alienation, broken relationships, misunderstandings, and immoral behavior. We want these to be driven out of the ruins they inhabit within us and to wander about and beg. We should extend no kindness to these interior forces, but hope that their days may indeed be few.

As Christians, we cannot pray this psalm against other people, but we can pray it against those interior demons that prevent us from being the people we know God wants us to be. The way to deal with psalms of vengeance is to turn them inward, and pray them against those forces of evil within us. The little ones that we want dashed against a rock in Psalm 137 are those petty prejudices and those puny jealousies that damage our relationships with others. This was not the original meaning of that psalm, but that is what it can mean to those of us who reject violence. It also reminds us of how irresponsibility and anger can lead to child abuse in our own time. That, too, can stimulate our prayer for suffering children.

We must not read the psalms self-righteously. Psalm 36 has a description of the wicked:

> There is no fear of God before their eyes.
> For they flatter themselves in their own eyes
> > that their iniquity cannot be found out and hated.
> The words of their mouths are mischief and deceit;
> > they have ceased to act wisely and do good.
> They plot mischief while on their beds;
> > they are set on a way that is not good;
> > they do not reject evil. (vv. 1–4)

We may read this psalm and think to ourselves that we know people like that. We wish they would straighten out their lives. But the psalm also challenges us to self-examination, what spiritual writers call examination of conscience. Does this description of evil apply to us in any way? Have we been guilty of mischief and deceit? Have we ceased to act wisely and do good? Do we think that our own iniquity cannot be found out? Such a reading of the psalm stimulates us to pray about our own human condition.

Psalm 136 is, in many ways, a beautiful psalm about God's providential care of Israel. It states something that God has done, and then has a repetitive refrain, "for his steadfast love endures forever." It begins with words of thanksgiving:

> O give thanks to the LORD, for he is good,
> > for his steadfast love endures forever.
> O give thanks to the God of gods,
> > for his steadfast love endures forever.
> O give thanks to the Lord of lords,
> > for his steadfast love endures forever. (vv. 1–3)

The psalm then shifts to God's acts of creation:

> Who by understanding made the heavens,
>   for his steadfast love endures forever;
> who spread out the earth on the waters,
>   for his steadfast love endures forever,
> who made the great lights,
>   for his steadfast love endures forever;
> the sun to rule over the day,
>   for his steadfast love endures forever;
> the moon and stars to rule over the night,
>   for his steadfast love endures forever. (vv. 5–9)

The psalm then takes up the story of Israel's exodus from Egypt:

> Who struck Egypt through their firstborn,
>   for his steadfast love endures forever;
> and brought Israel out from among them,
>   for his steadfast love endures forever;
> with a strong hand and an outstretched arm,
>   for his steadfast love endures forever;
> who divided the Red Sea in two,
>   for his steadfast love endures forever;
> and made Israel pass through the midst of it,
>   for his steadfast love endures forever. (vv. 10–14)

That is a familiar story to most of us. We can see the creation of the world and the liberation of slaves from Egypt as expressions of God's steadfast love. But then the psalm turns warlike. God is one

> who struck down great kings,
>   for his steadfast love endures forever;
> and killed famous kings,
>   for his steadfast love endures forever;
> Sihon, king of the Amorites,
>   for his steadfast love endures forever;

and Og, king of Bashan,
    for his steadfast love endures forever;
and gave their land as a heritage,
    for his steadfast love endures forever. (vv. 17–21)

The contrast between praising God for killing kings and Jesus' teaching in the Sermon on the Mount of nonviolence, turning the other cheek, and loving enemies raises questions for us. Can violence be an expression of God's steadfast love? If not, how do we pray this psalm?

What are the forces in your life that you want defeated? The pharaoh of hatred, the Sihon of uncontrollable anger, the Og of unreasonable jealousy? You could pray that God would help you overcome these foes, and you could have confidence that God would, "for his steadfast love endures forever." When we put ourselves in God's hands, when we are willing to give up our own selfishness and turn ourselves over to God's transforming mercy, that steadfast love of God can make us new people.

Psalm 136 celebrates this in its concluding verses.

It is he who remembered us in our low estate,
    for his steadfast love endures forever;
and rescued us from our foes,
    for his steadfast love endures forever;
who gives food to all flesh,
    for his steadfast love endures forever.
O give thanks to the God of heaven,
    for his steadfast love endures forever. (vv. 23–26)

Some of the psalms repulse us because of their violence, anger, and vengeful attitudes. Still, there is a reason they are in the Psalter, and it is not just to encourage nationalistic patriotism. Though they have been passed down to us for reasons we do not always know, they can be useful to us in our prayer lives if they force us to take a good look at our own attitudes and if we are able to pray them against those internal enemies that distort our personalities and cause us to be alienated from others. The psalmists may not have had this approach in mind when they wrote them, but now, several thousand years later, we can find them speaking to the universal human condition and giving us the language we need to pray about that condition.

8

Spirituality and Ethics

Bob and Martha belonged to a small prayer group that meant much to them. The group would gather every Thursday night in members' homes for a time of Bible reading and prayer. They prayed for sick friends, for people they knew who were facing divorce, for those whose children were in trouble. They would pray for their church, and they would give thanks for the middle-class lives they enjoyed. Although none of them were wealthy, they were comfortable, had reasonably secure jobs, and lived in what they thought was the right part of town.

On one occasion they began to talk about their church and, specifically, their minister. The conversation gradually degenerated into a very negative complaint session.

"He is talking too much about social issues," Bob said. "I don't come to church to be stirred up or made to feel guilty. I come to be comforted and find some peace."

"I agree," said another member. "I have enough stress in my life as it is. I don't need more in church."

"Yes," said Martha, "He keeps talking about God's concern for the poor. People like that would be uncomfortable in our church. They need to go somewhere else."

"If they would work, they wouldn't be poor," said another, ignoring the fact that a factory in the community that employed three hundred people had just shut down.

"We need to talk to our minister about this," offered Bob. "He needs to understand that we come to church to seek a relationship with God and personal salvation. He should focus more on that."

These people would benefit from praying the psalms, because the Psalter would not let them get away with a conversation like that. The psalms are filled with admonitions for social justice. As we pray for persons and situations, we are forced to face our ethical responsibilities. Ethical living is a major component of spirituality, and that is nowhere more clearly stated than in the psalms.

Early in the Psalter, in Psalm 5, we are told:

You are not a God who delights in wickedness;
  evil will not sojourn with you.
The boastful will not stand before your eyes;
  you hate all evildoers.
You destroy those who speak lies;
  the LORD abhors the bloodthirsty and deceitful.
    (vv. 4–6)

Psalm 9 makes clear God's judgment on evil:

He judges the world with righteousness;
  he judges the peoples with equity. (v. 8)

Perhaps Bob and Martha and their friends think that these verses only apply to personal moral lapses, such as lying, adultery, or cheating on your taxes. The question, of course, is what constitutes wickedness and evil in God's eyes. More things than we can imagine, I suspect, but the Psalter gives some basic guidelines on social justice issues.

One of the biggest concerns expressed in the Psalter is for widows, orphans, and strangers. For example, Psalm 10 reminds us that God has been "the helper of the orphan" (v. 14), and asks God "to do justice for the orphan and the oppressed" (v. 18). Psalm 82 likewise says, "Give justice to the weak and the orphan" (v. 3). Psalm 94 gives us a startling picture of injustice in ancient Israel when it complains about those who "kill the widow and the stranger, they murder the orphan" (v. 6). But Psalm 146 affirms,

The LORD watches over the strangers;
  he upholds the orphan and the widow,
  but the way of the wicked he brings to ruin. (v. 9)

Likewise, Psalm 68 describes God as "Father of orphans and protector of widows" (v. 5).

The poor, for whom Bob and Martha seem to show little sympathy, are also described in the psalms as objects of God's attention. The writer of Psalm 9 wants us to know that

The needy shall not always be forgotten,
  nor the hope of the poor perish forever. (v. 18)

Psalm 10 reports:

In arrogance the wicked persecute the poor—
>   let them be caught in the schemes they have
>   devised. (v. 2)
They lurk that they may seize the poor;
>   they seize the poor and drag them off in their net.
>   (v. 9)

The people in Bob and Martha's group might well give thought to how their own prosperity is built on the lives of the poor, those who work for a minimum wage, which does not begin to cover the cost of living; those whose low-paying jobs are subject to the whims of economic fluctuations; and those whose labor is needed only seasonally. They need to ponder Psalm 41:

Happy are those who consider the poor;
>   the LORD delivers them in the day of trouble.
The LORD protects them and keeps them alive;
>   they are called happy in the land. (vv. 1–2)

Such words are the opposite of a callous and judgmental attitude toward those who live on the underside of an affluent economy. The prayer group might pray Psalm 82:

Give justice to the weak and the orphan;
>   maintain the right of the lowly and the destitute.
Rescue the weak and the needy;
>   deliver them from the hand of the wicked. (vv. 3–4)

Psalm 140 affirms God's concern for the poor.

I know that the LORD maintains the cause of the needy,
>   and executes justice for the poor. (v. 12)

That should be a comforting thought to the prayer group, because economic conditions change, and forces over which the group members have no control could leave them in the category of poor and needy unexpectedly. Our social history contains many stories of prosperous people who lose everything.

Although to us the psalms seem full of violence, many psalms condemn it. Psalm 11 says that God "hates the lover of violence" (v. 5). Psalm 27 complains of those who "are breathing out violence" (v. 12), and the writer of Psalm 55 is upset at seeing "violence and strife in the city" (v. 9). Psalm 73 describes the wicked by saying, "violence covers them like a garment"(v. 6), and the next psalm, Psalm 74, calls on God to act because "the dark places of the land are full of the haunts of violence" (v. 20). Psalm 106 even makes reference to the violence of child sacrifice:

> they poured out innocent blood,
> > the blood of their sons and daughters,
> whom they sacrificed to the idols of Canaan. (v. 38)

However, it must be noted that the psalmist believed that this happened because the Israelites did not destroy the Canaanites when they took over the land. There seems to be no escape from violence. God has often been used to justify it.

The twentieth century has been described as the most violent in history: holocausts in Europe, Cambodia, and Rwanda; two World Wars and many other more local conflicts; revolutions in the Middle East and Africa; well-publicized violence in Northern Ireland, Bosnia, Serbia, Central America, Afghanistan, and many other places, such as breakaway republics in Russia. Violence is an integral part of human experience, but the psalmists make it clear that God opposes it. May we pray these prayers against violence fervently!

Greed is an ethical issue that the psalms take seriously. Psalm 57 speaks of those who "greedily devour human prey"

(v. 4), and Psalm 10 complains that "those greedy for gain curse and renounce the LORD" (v. 3). In answer to the question, "O LORD, who may abide in your tent?" the writer of Psalm 15 says, among other things, those who "do not take a bribe against the innocent" (v. 5). Psalm 26 is a prayer not to be swept away with sinners, "whose right hands are full of bribes" (v. 10).

Many of the psalms condemn deceitfulness. Psalm 24 is one example:

> Who shall ascend the hill of the LORD?
>   And who shall stand in his holy place?
> Those who have clean hands and pure hearts,
>   who do not lift up their souls to what is false,
>   and do not swear deceitfully. (vv. 3–4)

Psalm 50 has the voice of God saying:

> "You give your mouth free rein for evil,
>   and your tongue frames deceit.
> You sit and speak against your kin;
>   you slander your own mother's child…
> But now I rebuke you, and lay the charge before
>   you." (vv. 19–21)

Deceitfulness is a major concern in the psalms. Psalm 28 condemns those "who speak peace with their neighbors, while mischief is in their hearts" (v. 3).

Have you ever felt betrayed by a friend? Psalm 55 is a painful account of just that. The psalmist complains that he can deal with his enemies; it is a friend who is causing him misery.

> It is you, my equal,
>   my companion, my familiar friend,

with whom I kept pleasant company;
we walked in the house of God with the throng.
(vv. 13–14)

But the friend has been treacherous.

My companion laid hands on a friend
and violated a covenant with me
with speech smoother than butter,
but with a heart set on war;
with words that were softer than oil,
but in fact were drawn swords. (vv. 20–21)

Such folks will get what they deserve, the psalmist believed.

But you, O God, will cast them down
into the lowest pit;
the bloodthirsty and treacherous
shall not live out half their days. (v. 23)

Christians may have trouble with that harsh language, but it does reflect God's opposition to evil. Although the psalmist may not be able to resolve the issue, the psalm concludes with a positive word to God. "But I will trust in you" (v. 23). We cannot always control what our friends do, but we can put our trust in God.

Cast your burden on the LORD,
and he will sustain you. (v. 22)

Psalm 119 is the longest psalm in the Psalter, 176 verses. It is broken up into twenty-two eight-verse units. The psalm is a long prayer for faithfulness to the law of God, a law that may not always be easy either to understand or to keep. So the psalmist prays for the ability to keep God's commandments. It begins, like the Sermon on the Mount, with beatitudes.

Happy are those whose way is blameless,
who walk in the law of the LORD.
Happy are those who keep his decrees,
who seek him with their whole heart,
who also do no wrong,
but walk in his ways. (vv. 1–3)

Following the law of the Lord is the way to religious purity.

How can young people keep their way pure?
By guarding it according to your word. (v. 9)

The psalm makes clear the connection between moral living
and one's relationship with God.

With my whole heart I seek you;
do not let me stray from your commandments. (v. 10)

The writer believed that following God's commandments
led to deeper intimacy with God. There were many
additional benefits listed in the psalm:

I run the way of your commandments,
for you enlarge my understanding. (v. 32)
I find my delight in your commandments,
because I love them. (v. 47)
The law of your mouth is better to me
than thousands of gold and silver pieces. (v. 72)
If your law had not been my delight,
I would have perished in my misery.
I will never forget your precepts,
for by them you have given me life. (vv. 92–93)
Your commandment makes me wiser than my
enemies,
for it is always with me.
I have more understanding than all my teachers,
for your decrees are my meditation.

I understand more than the aged,
    for I keep your precepts. (vv. 98–100)
Through your precepts I get understanding;
    therefore I hate every false way.
Your word is a lamp to my feet
    and a light to my path. (vv. 104–105)

That is a rather amazing list. The law of God enlarges understanding so that the psalmist has a deeper understanding than teachers or the aged. It is life-giving, a source of wisdom. It is a guide that illuminates darkness. This particular psalm does not provide any specific ethical instructions, but it leads us to pray for faithfulness and obedience.

The very first psalm warns against keeping company with those who do evil:

Happy are those
    who do not follow the advice of the wicked,
or take the path that sinners tread,
    or sit in the seat of scoffers. (Ps. 1:1)

The writer of Psalm 94 had a profound sense that God knows the evil that we do:

Understand, O dullest of the people;
    fools, when will you be wise?
He who planted the ear, does he not hear?
He who formed the eye, does he not see?...
The LORD knows our thoughts,
    that they are but an empty breath. (vv. 8–11)

The same thought is expressed in Psalm 139:

O LORD, you have searched me and known me.
You know when I sit down and when I rise up;
    you discern my thoughts from far away.

You search out my path and my lying down,
and are acquainted with all my ways.
Even before a word is on my tongue,
O LORD, you know it completely. (vv. 1–4)

The psalms keep reminding us that regardless of our prejudice and hard-heartedness, God is deeply concerned for the poor, the neglected, the threatened, the victim of injustice, the marginalized. We would be wise to pray Psalm 141:

Set a guard over my mouth, O LORD;
keep watch over the door of my lips.
Do not turn my heart to any evil,
to busy myself with wicked deeds
in the company with those who work iniquity. (v. 3)

That is another version of "lead us not into temptation, and deliver us from evil." It not only speaks of the impact of evil on us, but warns us not to do evil to others. Before criticizing their pastor for his social justice preaching, Bob and Martha and their friends would do well to meditate on the psalms in this chapter.

9

Finding Christ in the Psalms

The psalmists knew nothing about Jesus of Nazareth, for the psalms were written before he appeared on the scene of history. The book of Psalms as we know it developed in stages from around the fifth to the second centuries B.C.E.[1] Nevertheless, the psalms are important to the New Testament. In his book *Out of the Depths: The Psalms Speak for Us Today,* Bernhard Anderson lists some ninety-nine passages in the psalms that are quoted or referred to in the New Testament,[2] emphasizing that many New Testament

---

[1]Bernhard W. Anderson, *Understanding the Old Testament,* 4th ed. (Englewood Cliffs, N.J.: Prentice-Hall, 1986), 545.
[2]Bernhard W. Anderson, *Out of the Depths: The Psalms Speak for Us Today,* rev. ed. (Philadelphia: Westminster Press, 1983), 243–45.

writers used images from the psalms to describe Jesus and explain who he was.

A number of psalms bring Jesus to mind, one such being Psalm 22:

> My God, my God, why have you forsaken me? (v. 1)

These are the words that the gospel writers Matthew and Luke have Jesus uttering from the cross. Perhaps one reason that we remember those words from the cross so well is that we have prayed them ourselves when things have not gone right for us. This is one point at which many of us can identify with Jesus. Other verses of that psalm are similar:

> All who see me mock at me;
>> they make mouths at me, they shake their heads;
> "Commit your cause to the LORD; let him deliver—
>> let him rescue the one in whom he delights!"
>> (vv. 7–8)

These words remind us of the mocking of Jesus and people telling him to save himself if he is the Son of God. It is easy to believe that the gospel writers also drew on the language of this psalm to describe Jesus' passion:

> A company of evildoers encircles me.
> My hands and feet have shriveled;
> I can count all my bones.
> They stare and gloat over me;
> they divide my clothes among themselves,
>> and for my clothing they cast lots. (vv. 16–18)

It would be well nigh impossible for a Christian to pray this psalm without thinking about Christ. That may not have been what the psalmist had in mind, but what we bring to the psalms affects how we pray them.[3]

Psalm 69 contains another passion image:

> They gave me poison for food,
> and for my thirst they gave me vinegar to drink.
> (v. 21)

Psalm 31 contains the words we identify with Jesus' death, "Into your hands I commit my spirit" (v. 5). There are many other such images in the Psalter. For example, Psalm 2:

> He said to me, "You are my son;
> today I have begotten you." (v. 7)

Psalm 23 reminds us of Jesus as the good shepherd. Psalm 45, a wedding psalm, was often seen by medieval writers, who used allegory as an interpretative device, as a psalm about Christ:

> You are the most handsome of men;
> grace is poured upon your lips;
> therefore God has blessed you forever. (v. 2)

Such interpreters saw the church as the bride of Christ and this psalm as describing the relationship that ought to exist between the church and Christ.

> Hear, O daughter, consider and incline your ear;
> forget your people and your father's house,
> and the king will desire your beauty. (v. 10)

Medieval mystics often interpreted the images of lover and beloved in the Song of Solomon as representing Christ and

---

[3]Walter Brueggemann, *Praying the Psalms* (Winona, Minn.: Saint Mary's Press, 1982).

the church, so it was natural that Psalm 45 would be understood this way.

Psalm 72 is a psalm of royal or kingly images. We may not live under a king in the United States, but we are certainly familiar with the image of kingship and know that it has often been applied to God. There are churches that have in their names the words "Christ the King," followed by a denominational designation. The opening words of this psalm make us think of God the Father and Christ the Son.

> Give the king your justice, O God,
>   and your righteousness to a king's son.
> May he judge your people with righteousness,
>   and your poor with justice...
> May he defend the cause of the poor of the people,
>   give deliverance to the needy,
>   and crush the oppressor. (vv. 1–4)

These words also remind us of Christ as the final judge of all things, whose justice is tempered with mercy and who cares about the needy and the oppressed.

> For he delivers the needy when they call,
>   the poor and those who have no helper.
> He has pity on the weak and the needy,
>   and saves the lives of the needy.
> From oppression and violence he redeems their life;
>   and precious is their blood in his sight.
>   (vv. 12–14)

Jesus' care for the poor, the demented, the sick and disabled, and the oppressed, as well as those who wanted to live faithfully and sought him out with questions, come to mind through these words. Using such psalms, our own prayers become self-examinations of our attitude toward the marginalized, the unlovely, and those who need signs of love and care, which they do not often find in good, religious people.

Another familiar New Testament image is found in Psalm 118:

> The stone that the builders rejected
> has become the chief cornerstone. (v. 22)

After telling the story of the vineyard where the wicked tenants killed the owner's son, Jesus said, "Have you never read in the scriptures, 'The stone that the builders rejected has become the cornerstone?'" (Mt. 21:42).[4] In Acts, Peter is quoted: "This Jesus is 'the stone that was rejected by you, the builders; it has become the cornerstone'" (Acts 4:11). Ephesians 2:20 says "with Christ Jesus himself as the cornerstone." Finally, 1 Peter 2:7 contains the same quotation from Psalm 118.

Psalm 137 is one of the few psalms that scholars believe we can come close to dating accurately. After the people of Judah had been conquered and taken in exile to Babylonia, they lamented,

> If I forget you, O Jerusalem,
> let my right hand wither! (v. 5)

Their identity was bound up in the city of Jerusalem, the capital and religious center of their defeated nation. But for Christians, Jerusalem is the place where Christ died for our sins, something we never want to forget, for our identity is bound up in that cross at Golgotha.

Is Christ present in the Psalter? Literally, no. However, many images in the psalms bring Christ into our minds, stimulate our memory of Christ, and move us into new directions of prayer.

---

[4]See also Mark 12:10 and Luke 20:17.

Psalms around the Clock

When is the right time to pray? The answer to that question depends on many individual circumstances. As mentioned in chapter 1, some of us are morning people, and some are night people. If we live with others, some of us might prefer to rise early, before others are awake, in order to find time to pray. Others might prefer to wait until after the rest of the household has gone to bed. Some of us may be able to find free moments during the day. The psalms can be prayed at any time, but many of them make reference to certain times of the day, indicating when they may have originally been used.

The first psalm that mentions a time of day is Psalm 5.

O LORD, in the morning you hear my voice;
in the morning I plead my case to you, and
watch. (v. 3)

In Psalm 108, the psalmist writes of beginning the morning with prayer.

My heart is steadfast, O God, my heart is steadfast;
I will sing and make melody.
Awake, my soul!
Awake, O harp and lyre!
I will awake the dawn. (vv. 1–2)

We awaken our bodies in the morning. Often we hear the awakening of the world: the sounds of birds and other creatures, as well as the movement of people getting up and going to work. We see the sunrise, the fading darkness, everything involved with the beginning of the day. The psalmist urges us to awaken our souls as well as our bodies.

In the Benedictine monastic tradition a monk's prayer life is built around chanting the psalms in services called Divine Offices. Monks call this *opus dei,* the work of God. Psalm 119 sets the schedule for the Divine Offices. It calls for prayer at midnight, "At midnight I rise to praise you, because of your righteous ordinances" (v. 62); in the predawn, "I rise before dawn and cry for help; I put my hope in your words" (v. 147); seven times a day, "Seven times a day I praise you for your righteous ordinances" (v. 164).

The Rule of Saint Benedict, the most widely used monastic rule in the Middle Ages and still much in use today, followed the instruction of this psalm and prescribed seven times of prayer each day plus night prayer. Benedict's schedule looked like this:

Vigils—night prayer

Lauds—prayer of praise, usually before dawn

Prime—prayer at the first hour of the day, our 6:00 a.m.

Terce—prayer at the third hour of the day, our
    9:00 a.m.

Sext—prayer at the sixth hour of the day, our noon

None—prayer at the ninth hour of the day, our
    3:00 p.m.

Vespers—prayer in the late afternoon

Compline—prayer before going to bed, which
    "completes" the day

The schedule provided a rhythm for the main elements of the monk's life: prayer, work, and *lectio divina,* or divine reading. (See chapter 12 for an explanation of this practice.)

In more recent years the office of Prime has been dropped, and in many places there are only night, morning, midday, and evening prayers. In some religious communities there are only morning and evening prayers. Still, the principle is the same: time is sanctified by periodic prayer spread throughout the day.

This schedule is unrealistic for the average layperson, but the principle is the same: sanctify the day with prayer whenever possible. For most people, morning and evening would be realistic. For many once a day would be an accomplishment. Whatever you can do, it is the regular turning of your attention to God that forms you as a Christian person and helps to break through that wall of distractions that keeps you from sensing the Divine Presence.

A number of psalms make reference to the cycle of day and night. Psalm 30 speaks of a common cycle of human experience of suffering and healing:

> Weeping may linger for the night,
>> but joy comes with the morning. (v. 5)

Psalm 55 expresses the faith that God hears persistent prayer:

> Evening and morning and at noon
>> I utter my complaint and moan,
>> and he will hear my voice. (v. 17)

Psalm 92 urges morning and evening prayer:

> It is good to give thanks to the LORD,
>> to sing praises to your name, O Most High;
> to declare your steadfast love in the morning,
>> and your faithfulness by night.
>>> (vv. 1–2)

Psalm 5 has already been mentioned as a morning psalm. Psalm 59, a psalm calling for deliverance from enemies, concludes,

> I will sing of your might;
>> I will sing aloud of your steadfast love in the
>>> morning. (v. 16)

Psalm 88, also the psalm of a deeply troubled person, adds this line:

> I, O LORD, cry out to you;
>> in the morning my prayer comes before you.
>>> (v. 13)

Another morning psalm, Psalm 90, pleads for the love of God:

> Satisfy us in the morning with your steadfast love,
>> so that we may rejoice and be glad all our days.
>>> (v. 14)

A similar prayer is found in Psalm 143:

> Let me hear of your steadfast love in the morning,
>   for in you I put my trust. (v. 8)

Night is a time that many people find appealing for prayer, for we often struggle with difficult issues at that time. An image that has often been used for spiritual struggle is "the dark night of the soul," made famous by Saint John of the Cross, a sixteenth-century Spanish mystic. The writer of Psalm 6, obviously struggling with such a dark night, complained,

> I am weary with my moaning;
>   every night I flood my bed with tears. (v. 6)

Similar sentiments are expressed in Psalm 77:

> In the day of my trouble I seek the Lord;
>   in the night my hand is stretched out without
>   wearying;
>   my soul refuses to be comforted.
> I think of God, and I moan;
>   I meditate, and my spirit faints. (vv. 2–3)

The psalmist gives us language for prayer as we wrestle with doubt and uncertainty of faith:

> I commune with my heart in the night;
>   I meditate and search my spirit. (v. 6)

Psalm 17 speaks of God visiting us by night, and Psalm 63 prays:

> my mouth praises you with joyful lips
> when I think of you on my bed
>   and meditate on you in the watches of the night.
>   (vv. 5–6)

Psalm 88 is one of the most depressing in the Psalter. The psalmist lists a host of troubles: God's wrath seems to have overwhelmed; companions have shunned; and God does not seem to respond. But still the psalmist prays:

> When, at night, I cry out in your presence,
> let my prayer come before you;
>> incline your ear to my cry. (vv. 1–2)

Prayer morning and evening is a good discipline, a good way to bracket the day, no matter what is happening in your life, and a number of psalms are appropriate for praying at the end of the day. Psalm 4 is often sung in monasteries right before the monks go to bed. It is a psalm of thanksgiving for the goodness of God, but also advises:

> When you are disturbed, do not sin;
>> ponder it on your beds, and be silent. (v. 4)

It concludes with:

> I will both lie down and sleep in peace;
>> for you alone, O LORD, make me lie down in
>> safety. (v. 8)

The other psalm that is sung by monks at the end of the day is Psalm 91:

> You will not fear the terror of the night,
>> or the arrow that flies by day,
> or the pestilence that stalks in darkness,
>> or the destruction that wastes at noonday.
>> (vv. 5–6)

Another evening psalm is Psalm 16:

> I bless the LORD who gives me counsel;
>> in the night also my heart instructs me. (v. 7)

The last evening psalm is Psalm 134.

> Come bless the LORD, all you servants of the LORD,
>   who stand by night in the house of the LORD! (v. 1)

No matter when we pray the psalms, we can be sure that someone, somewhere in the world, is also praying them. We join them in a heavenly chorus, praising God together.

11

Praising God with the Psalms

More than anything else, the Psalter is a book of praise. In trying to categorize the psalms for chapter divisions, I discovered that psalms of praise constituted by far the largest category. That is as it should be. There is nothing more important in our prayer lives than to praise God, the God who gave us life and gives us countless blessings, most of which we don't even notice.

Psalm 8 is a psalm of thanksgiving for the natural world and the gift of humanity. It is bracketed by the first and last verses:

O LORD, our Sovereign,
　　how majestic is your name in all the earth!

Psalm 18 expresses the same enthusiasm:

> I will extol you, O LORD, among the nations,
>   and sing praises to your name. (v. 49)

Praise is understood in a variety of ways and for a variety of reasons in the Psalter. Some of the psalms speak of all nature praising God, as in Psalm 19:

> The heavens are telling the glory of God;
>   and the firmament proclaims his handiwork. (v. 1)

Psalm 96 makes reference to nature's praising God, who is coming to judge the earth:

> Let the heavens be glad, and let the earth rejoice;
>   let the sea roar, and all that fills it;
>   let the field exult, and everything in it.
> Then shall all the trees of the forest sing for joy
>   before the LORD; for he is coming,
>   for he is coming to judge the earth. (vv. 11–13)

Similar images are used in Psalm 98:

> Let the sea roar, and all that fills it;
>   the world and those who live in it.
> Let the floods clap their hands;
>   let the hills sing together for joy
> at the presence of the LORD, for he is coming
>   to judge the earth. (vv. 7–9)

The Psalter ends with several thunderous songs of praise. Psalm 148 again tells of all nature praising God:

> Praise him, sun and moon;
>   praise him, all you shining stars!
> Praise him, you highest heavens,
>   and you waters above the heavens!

Let them praise the name of the LORD,
> for he commanded and they were created.
>> (vv. 3–5)

Praise the LORD from the earth,
> you sea monsters and all deeps,

fire and hail, snow and frost,
> stormy wind fulfilling his command!

Mountains and all hills,
> fruit trees and all cedars!

Wild animals and all cattle,
> creeping things and flying birds! (vv. 7–10)

Let them praise the name of the LORD,
> for his name alone is exalted;
>> his glory is above earth and heaven. (v. 13)

In addition to nature engaging in praise, many psalms offer praise for nature itself, as in Psalm 65:

Praise is due to you, O God, in Zion. (v. 1)

You visit the earth and water it,
> you greatly enrich it;

the river of God is full of water;
> you provide the people with grain,
> for so you have prepared it.

You water its furrows abundantly,
> settling its ridges,

softening it with showers,
> and blessing its growth. (vv. 9–10)

The pastures of the wilderness overflow,
> the hills gird themselves with joy,

the meadows clothe themselves with flocks,
> the valleys deck themselves with grain,
> they shout and sing together for joy. (vv. 12–13)

Psalm 104 expresses similar reasons for praise:

You make springs gush forth in the valleys;
  they flow between the hills,
giving drink to every wild animal;
  the wild asses quench their thirst. (vv. 10–11)
You cause the grass to grow for the cattle,
  and plants for people to use,
to bring forth food from the earth,
  and wine to gladden the human heart.
    (vv. 14–15)
O LORD, how manifold are your works!
  In wisdom you have made them all. (v. 24)

Many of the psalms praise God for military victory.
Psalm 47 is an example:

Clap your hands, all you peoples;
  shout to God with loud songs of joy.
For the LORD, the Most High, is awesome,
  a great king over all the earth.
He subdued peoples under us,
  and nations under our feet. (vv. 1–3)

Likewise in Psalm 98:

O sing to the LORD a new song,
  for he has done marvelous things.
His right hand and his holy arm
  have gotten him victory.
The LORD has made known his victory;
  he has revealed his vindication in the sight of the
    nations. (vv. 1–2)

Psalm 105 is a long summary of the history of Israel. It
begins with the patriarchs—Abraham, Isaac, and Jacob—
and the promise of the land of Canaan. Then it tells the

story of the sojourn in Egypt and the exodus. We are told about the plagues, the wilderness wandering, and finally the conquering of the land:

> So he brought his people out with joy,
>   his chosen ones with singing.
> He gave them the land of the nations,
>   and they took possession of the wealth of the
>   peoples,
> that they might keep his statutes
>   and observe his laws.
> Praise the LORD! (vv. 43–45)

The story is told again in Psalm 135:

> He struck down many nations
>   and killed mighty kings—
> Sihon, king of the Amorites,
>   and Og, king of Bashan,
>   and all the kingdoms of Canaan—
> and gave their land as a heritage,
>   a heritage to his people Israel. (vv. 10–12)

You might not think that prayers for military victory can contribute much to your prayer life. However, if we internalize these psalms, they can become important prayers for us. We pray that God would defeat Og, our own selfishness; Sihon, our prejudices; and pharaoh, the injustice that we see all around us. We seem unable to overcome some personality traits that defeat us: jealousy, resentment of others, ego needs that have to be satisfied, the lack of a capacity to love. These are the nations we pray for God to defeat for us that we might live in a new land of love, mercy, compassion, and justice. We need many interior victories, and only the grace of God can help us win those battles.

Several of the psalms praise God for answering prayer, as in Psalm 34:

> O magnify the LORD with me,
>   and let us exalt his name together.
> I sought the LORD, and he answered me,
>   and delivered me from all my fears.
> Look to him, and be radiant;
>   so your faces shall never be ashamed.
> This poor soul cried, and was heard by the LORD,
>   and was saved from every trouble. (vv. 3–6)

Psalm 138 expresses similar sentiments.

> I give you thanks, O LORD, with my whole heart;
>   before the gods I sing your praise. (v. 1)
> On the day I called, you answered me,
>   you increased the strength of my soul. (v. 3)

The love and faithfulness of God are the subject of several psalms of praise. Psalm 48, which is actually a psalm of victory in war, also contains a loftier element:

> We ponder your steadfast love, O God,
>   in the midst of your temple.
> Your name, O God, like your praise,
>   reaches to the ends of the earth. (vv. 9–10)

The same note is sounded in Psalm 57:

> Your steadfast love is as high as the heavens;
>   your faithfulness extends to the clouds.
>   (v. 10)

Psalm 92 offers a similar prayer:

> It is good to give thanks to the LORD,
>   to sing praises to your name, O Most High;

to declare your steadfast love in the morning,
  and your faithfulness by night. (vv. 1–2)

The shortest psalm, 117, also emphasizes God's faithfulness:

Praise the LORD, all you nations!
  Extol him, all you peoples!
For great is his steadfast love toward us,
  and the faithfulness of the LORD endures forever.
Praise the LORD!

There are times when all of us live in fear of something
or someone. Psalm 56 is an appropriate prayer in that
situation:

O Most High, when I am afraid,
  I put my trust in you.
In God, whose word I praise,
  in God I trust; I am not afraid;
  what can flesh do to me? (vv. 2–4)

In chapter 6 we looked at psalms that we can use when
we need to confess our sins to God. Confession, however,
is not enough by itself. We must also thank God for the
gospel promise of forgiveness. Psalm 65 gives us the
appropriate language.

Praise is due to you, O God, in Zion;
  and to you shall vows be performed,
    O you who answer prayer!
To you all flesh shall come.
When deeds of iniquity overwhelm us,
  you forgive our transgressions. (vv. 1–3)

The same basic prayer is found in Psalm 103:

Bless the LORD, O my soul,
  and do not forget all his benefits—

who forgives all your iniquity,
who heals all your diseases. (vv. 2–3)

One prayer that each of us ought to pray is a prayer of thanksgiving for our own lives. Psalm 100 reminds us that we exist because of the creative action of God:

Know that the LORD is God.
It is he that made us, and we are his;
we are his people, and the sheep of his pasture. (v. 3)

Several psalms offer praise to God for what God has done. Psalm 145 gives a long list of the blessings received from God:

Every day I will bless you,
and praise your name forever and ever.
Great is the LORD, and greatly to be praised;
his greatness is unsearchable.
One generation shall laud your works to another,
and shall declare your mighty acts.
On the glorious splendor of your majesty,
and on your wondrous works, I will meditate.
The might of your awesome deeds shall be
proclaimed. (vv. 2–6)

And what are these awesome deeds on which the psalmist will meditate?

The LORD is gracious and merciful,
slow to anger and abounding in steadfast love. (v. 8)
The LORD is faithful in all his words,
and gracious in all his deeds.
The LORD upholds all who are falling,
and raises up all how are bowed down. (vv. 13–14)

You open your hand,
> satisfying the desire of every living thing. (v. 16)
The Lord is near to all who call on him. (v. 18)

We are all blessed with so much. We may not have nearly all we want, but we have the presence of God in our lives. That is the promise of the Psalter, and it is the promise of the Christian gospel. That, in itself, should be enough to evoke our deepest praise.

Everyone who knows and loves God would hope for what is expressed in Psalm 66:

> "All the earth worships you;
>> they sing praises to you,
>> sing praises to your name." (v. 4)

Psalm 67 is a prayer for God's blessing. It has a chorus that is repeated twice.

> Let the peoples praise you, O God;
>> let all the peoples praise you. (vv. 3, 5)

The final two psalms in the Psalter tell us how to praise. For Israel, it was not just an interior or mental activity. Praise involved singing, dancing, and playing musical instruments. Psalm 149 is a psalm of military victory, but it shows that the people knew how to praise:

> Let Israel be glad in its Maker;
>> let the children of Zion rejoice in their King.
> Let them praise his name with dancing,
>> making melody to him with tambourine and lyre.
> For the Lord takes pleasure in his people.
>> (vv. 2–4)

Finally, the last psalm, 150, encourages exultant praise.

Praise him with trumpet sound;
  praise him with lute and harp!
Praise him with tambourine and dance;
  praise him with strings and pipe!
Praise him with clanging cymbals;
  praise him with loud clashing cymbals!
Let everything that breathes praise the LORD!
Praise the LORD! (vv. 3–6)

12

Lectio Divina

There is an ancient spiritual practice in the church called *lectio divina*. These Latin words literally mean "divine reading." In its classic form it is the practice of reading a passage of scripture devotionally, listening specifically for what the Holy Spirit is saying to you.

Lectio divina differs from study in the scholarly sense. There are times when you would want to study the psalms as ancient literature by looking at their literary forms, their linguistic characteristics, their historical context, their place in the canon. You might want to study the nature of the text and try to arrive at some conclusions about authorship and date. You might consider such questions as, How did Israel use these psalms? What impact did they have on the nation? What were the writers' sources of information? Were they written at the time of the events described, or were they later reflections on what happened? This is essential information for understanding what the psalms meant to ancient Israel, to their intended audiences. Such study is foundational to a deep and responsible knowledge of scripture.

Lectio divina does not discount the value of that kind of scholarship, but it has a different agenda. Is the Holy Spirit saying something to you as you read carefully the words of scripture, in this case the psalms? Some have referred to it as "reading with the heart."

Church history is full of conversion stories about people who just happened to read or hear read a passage of scripture at a crucial time, and their lives were radically changed. Augustine, in a moment of disgust with his own life, read a passage in Romans and was finally converted. Benedict heard read in church the words of Jesus, "Take what you have, sell it, give to the poor, and come follow me." That conversion ultimately led to the founding of Benedictine monasticism. John Wesley went reluctantly to a church meeting on Aldersgate Street, and while hearing read comments by Martin Luther on Paul's letter to the Romans, he felt his heart "strangely warmed" and had a new certainty that his sins had been forgiven.

Such sudden conversions may be out of the ordinary, but in these cases the Holy Spirit revealed something to these people that was life-changing. Perhaps you will not have such a radical experience, but in practicing *lectio divina* you may gain new insight and a new awareness of the Holy in your life. You may read a passage that you have read many, many times and on some occasion see something in it that you never saw before.

Three things are involved in *lectio divina:* a scripture text, you, and the Holy Spirit. You read a passage and listen to see if the Holy Spirit is going to reveal anything to you. You must allow for time; *lectio divina* is not the kind of reading that can be rushed. You need to listen for a time—fifteen, twenty minutes or more, whatever you can manage—and carry that text with you throughout the day's activities. But the key is having the text in your mind and listening prayerfully in the faith that the Holy Spirit is present in the experience. You read slowly and carefully and listen in the context of the presence of the Divine, allowing yourself to be transformed by the text. Some days not much may happen, and some days you may be surprised by a rich experience of insight and awareness.

A twelfth-century Carthusian monk, known to us by the name Guigo II, wrote a delightful little book called *The Ladder of Monks.* In it he described a four-step process using the Latin words *lectio, meditatio, oratio,* and *contemplatio.*

Lectio was the reading of scripture. Reading a passage and getting it firmly in your mind leads you to the second rung of the ladder, *meditatio,* or meditation. Here you ponder the passage, thinking about how it relates to your life, mulling over any insight you may receive. This activity moves you to *oratio,* or prayer. Now you pray about what you have gained from that passage, how that truth needs to be integrated into your life, what the sources of resistance may be, and how much you need God's grace in order to be faithful. Finally, prayer may lead to *contemplatio,* or contemplation. In the literature of Christian spirituality contemplation specifically means an awareness of God, an encounter with God, a sense of spiritual union with God. That may be just a fleeting moment, but if it occurs, it will have such power that you will never be quite the same again.

Take, for example, the first verses of Psalm 130.

Out of the depths I cry to you, O LORD.
Lord, hear my voice.

That is a nice introduction to a prayer. Of course you hope the Lord will hear you. You want God to hear you. Does praying mean that you are afraid God may not hear you, so in this prayer you demand a hearing? "Lord, hear my voice!" Perhaps what is happening here is that the Holy Spirit is telling you that God wants you to ask for a hearing; God wants to be called upon. But you don't demand. You approach God in fear and trembling; you don't assume anything. But you hope that your voice matters to God and that you will be heard. Otherwise, why would you be given the words to pray in scripture?

"Out of the depths, I cry to you, O LORD." Out of the depths, out of the depths, out of the depths. There is a phrase to ponder. What depths are we referring to? The depths of despair, the depths of profound joy, the depths of our heart? Depths.

So we begin to meditate on it. How superficial is your life? Does your life simply float along the trivialities? Do you think very deeply about God, or do you allow yourself to be controlled by the superficial values of an acquisitive culture? What is really important to you: your faith, your material possessions, your social status, your influence? Do you live by those deeper values of mercy, compassion, love, and faith, or do you live by values that have no lasting or eternal value?

Depths. Out of the depths. Are you ready to probe the very depths of your being, or are you afraid that when you go down there you will find demons that you have repressed? If you think deeply about yourself, will you find out things that you don't like and would rather not face? The Holy

Spirit may have given you more to think about than you bargained for.

The meditation begs for prayer. O God, how do I plunge into my depths? What do I have to do to look deeply within myself? Help me to evaluate my life honestly. Protect me from trivial values that would distract me from you. Hear my voice, O God, as I struggle with the demons that lurk in my depths, threatening to come to the surface and reveal who I am. But if you are present in my depths, help me to know that. I want to know you, God, for you have called me to prayer.

Will there be any *contemplatio?* Will you sense God's presence? That depends on the Holy Spirit, but part of the issue is your willingness to listen for and to the Spirit. You may take this passage and have a completely different experience than the one just described. I hope you will, for that was just a construct to illustrate the possibilities.

The psalms are so rich and virtually inexhaustible in their meaning. You may read the same one many times, yet one day something new will come into your mind. The efficacy of *lectio divina* depends in part on your willingness to trust the Holy Spirit, a faith that in these words of scripture God has something new to reveal to you.

Epilogue

I am really sorry, God, but I just don't feel like praying tonight. I have had a very busy day. I am dead tired and emotionally exhausted. I know I have committed myself to praying the psalms every day, but sometimes I don't, and today feels like one of those days. It would just be a relief if I were to decide that tonight I am not going to do it and go on to something else. But then there is that nagging feeling: I didn't keep my commitment. But more than that, I may have missed some gift you were going to give me today, some fresh insight that you know I need.

So I'll do it, but this time it will probably be an empty exercise, and the only good thing about it will be that I can say I have done it. Does that mean anything to you? Is it better to just go through the motions than not do anything at all, or is that just hypocritical? I know Trappist monks who pray the psalms together seven times a day. Does it always mean something to them? Do they sometimes just go through the motions? Do they find reasons for not showing up for community prayer? I have a lot of things I want to get done tonight, one of which is just to relax, but I'll put them off for a few minutes. How long do you expect me to pray tonight? Is this one of those times when some feeling will kick in and I will wait on you in silence for a long time, or can I get by with reading a few psalms quickly?

All right, here I am at my desk. I open my journal where I write down psalm verses that seem to speak to me, and open my Bible to the Psalter and start.

Psalm 49:

> Why should I fear in times of trouble,
>> when the iniquity of my persecutors surrounds
>> me? (v. 5)

That doesn't mean anything to me. I don't feel persecuted right now. There have been times when I have in the past, when people deliberately misinterpreted me and made me out to be the bad guy. But that was long ago. Right now things are going well for me. I'm happy with my life. I don't really feel that I have any enemies, although there may be some of which I am not aware. So what good does that verse do me?

> When we look at the wise, they die;
>> fool and dolt perish together
>> and leave their wealth to others.
> Their graves are their homes forever. (vv. 10–11)

Well, yes, I know death lies ahead. Now that I am retired, I think about it a lot. How long do I have? What will the experience be like? How much will I have to suffer? How much will my family have to suffer? Is there really life after death?

> But God will ransom my soul from the power of
>   Sheol,
>   for he will receive me. (v. 15)

That is a comforting thought. Will you really receive me? If you don't, what will happen to me? Will I just cease to exist, or will my personhood somehow survive?

> When they die they will carry nothing away;
>   their wealth will not go down after them.
>   (v. 17)

There is that wealth issue again. One of the things I wanted to do tonight was get on the Internet and check my investments. The stock market hasn't been very good lately. Do I have enough wealth to survive? I don't want to be a burden to my children; I sure don't want to go on welfare. I am awfully preoccupied with money matters. But it doesn't seem to matter to you. Do you know something about my life that I don't know?

Psalm 50:

> Our God comes and does not keep silence,
>   before him is a devouring fire,
>   and a mighty tempest all around him. (v. 3)

You are far too silent for me, O God. I believe that you come, but I don't see any devouring fire or mighty tempest. Am I missing something? I wish you would burn up and devour all the evil in the world, the suffering, the violence, the injustice, human insensitivity, and selfishness. But I don't see that happening.

The psalm says that you don't want animal sacrifices, since you own the whole creation anyway. You want a sacrifice of thanksgiving. Well, I can offer that. In spite of all the things that are wrong with the world, I am in pretty good shape: a wonderful family, reasonable financial security, many good friends, a church that I love. I don't need more than that, and I am profoundly thankful. I don't know why I have been so blessed when I could be a victim of famine in Africa, a victim of violence in some war-torn country, a political prisoner being tortured somewhere, or the child of an abusive parent. But I am not, and I am thankful, and I hope you hear that and know how profoundly sincere I am on that point.

I dread Psalm 51:

Have mercy on me, O God,
    according to your steadfast love;
according to your abundant mercy,
    blot out my transgressions.
Wash me thoroughly from my iniquity,
    and cleanse me from my sin.
For I know my transgressions,
    and my sin is ever before me. (vv. 1–3)

Why do I have to keep being reminded of that? I have done hurtful things to people; I have lied; I have been insensitive; and I sometimes have felt superior to others. I have walked by on the other side when someone needed me. Why can't I forget those things, put them behind me, and move on? But you won't let me, will you? You try to keep me humble by reminding me of my imperfections. So I have to pray this psalm. It brings up that underside of my soul that I wish was not there.

Create in me a clean heart, O God,
    and put a new and right spirit within me.
Do not cast me away from your presence,
    and do not take your holy spirit from me.
        (vv. 10–11)

Please, O God, put a right spirit in me. Make me a better person. I know my weaknesses, but you know them better than I. I would give anything if they were not there. Only your grace overcomes them.

Psalm 52:

Why do you boast, O mighty one,
    of mischief done against the godly?
    All day long you are plotting destruction.
Your tongue is like a sharp razor,
    you worker of treachery.
You love evil more than good,
    and lying more than speaking the truth. (vv. 1–3)

Am I really that bad? Do I ignore you that much? Sure, some people are like that, but am I? God, these psalms make me think things I don't want to think about. They make me look at my life. They set standards too high for me to reach.

But I am like a green olive tree
    in the house of God.
I trust in the steadfast love of God
    forever and ever. (v. 8)

That's how I want to be, God. I want to trust you like the person who wrote this psalm. Help me be that kind of person, because I want to be better than I am. I want to be capable of loving everyone and I want the moral courage to do your will.

Psalm 53:

Fools say in their hearts, "There is no God." (v. 1)

Yes, that is foolish. I already read this psalm. Psalm 14 is the same thing. Why is it there twice? Is it so you remind us more than once that it is foolish to say you do not exist? I know you exist. I have my doubts from time to time; you know that. There are times when I seek your presence, and you don't seem to be there, but I know you really are. But then there are times when your presence is so obvious that it always takes me by surprise. Why won't you come when I call? Do I always have to struggle with faith, and then be surprised when you do something? Do I make faith difficult when it is really easy? I see people whose faith is so sure and certain, but I just know that they don't see the problems I do. Otherwise they would be less certain. But maybe they struggle more than I realize.

God, this prayer time has been good for me. It was hard to get into it, but once I began praying these psalms, I knew that you were present.

O God, wherever you are, may your name be praised and honored everywhere.

May your rule over all human life become a reality, and may your will for us be done here where we live as it is wherever you live.

O God, you have given me daily bread in abundance. I eat far too much of it and am fat and overweight when there are those in this community, not to mention the world, who do not have enough to eat. Grant them their daily bread, and help me see ways I can provide it.

Forgive me, God, for all the dumb, stupid, insensitive things I do to others, and help me to forgive those who do dumb, stupid, insensitive things to me.

Help me, God, not to be tempted, and protect me from the powers of evil that make their way through this world and reside in too many human hearts.

For I do believe that ultimately you rule over all things, that you have all the final power, and may the glory be yours, now and forever. Amen.